The Ultimate AI Toolbox: Essential Tools & Frameworks for Building, Deploying, and Scaling AI Solutions

A Comprehensive Guide to the Best Tools for AI Development, From Model Training to Deployment and Optimization

Introduction

Artificial Intelligence (AI) is revolutionizing industries, automating tasks, and creating intelligent systems that can reason, learn, and adapt. Mastering AI and AI agent development requires a deep understanding of programming languages, machine learning frameworks, cloud computing, and MLOps (Machine Learning Operations).

This guide is designed for both beginners and professionals, offering a structured approach to mastering the key tools and technologies in AI development. Whether you want to build chatbots, autonomous systems, or optimize deep learning models,

1

this guide will help you navigate the landscape of AI programming effectively.

In this book, you will learn:

+ The best programming languages for AI development.

+ Frameworks and libraries used for AI and machine learning.

+ Tools for training and deploying AI agents.

+ Cloud and edge computing solutions for AI.

+ MLOps strategies for scaling AI models in production.

By the end of this guide, you'll have a clear roadmap to mastering AI technologies and developing intelligent agents that can interact, learn, and make decisions.

Chapter 1: Programming Languages & Frameworks for AI Development

Choosing the right programming language is the first step in AI development. Each language has its strengths and use cases, and understanding them will help you select the best tool for your AI projects.

1.1 Python – The Primary Language for AI

Why Python?
Python is the most widely used language in AI and machine learning due to its simplicity, vast libraries, and strong community support.

+ **Easy to Learn** – Python's simple syntax makes it beginner-friendly.
+ **Extensive AI Libraries** – TensorFlow, PyTorch, scikit-learn, and NumPy streamline AI development.
+ **Great for AI Agents** – Frameworks like LangChain help in building conversational AI models.
+ **Supports Deep Learning** – Used in training neural networks and computer vision applications.

Example Use Case:

- Developing a chatbot using Python's **NLTK (Natural Language Toolkit)** and **OpenAI's GPT models**.
- Training a deep learning model for image recognition with **TensorFlow/Keras**.

Getting Started with Python for AI:

1. Install Python (latest stable version).
2. Use package managers like pip or conda to install AI libraries.
3. Practice with small projects like image classification or simple chatbots.

1.2 C++ – High-Performance AI & Autonomous Systems

C++ is known for its **speed and efficiency**, making it a preferred choice for performance-critical AI applications.

+ **Used in AI for gaming** – Game engines like Unreal Engine use C++ for AI-driven NPC behavior.
+ **Great for Autonomous Systems** – Self-driving cars and robotics rely on C++ for real-time processing.
+ **Optimized for AI acceleration** – Works with **CUDA** for GPU computing.

Example Use Case:

- AI in self-driving cars, where C++ is used to process sensor data and make real-time decisions.
- Building high-performance AI models using **TensorRT** for fast inference.

Getting Started with C++ for AI:

1. Learn C++ basics (OOP, memory management, concurrency).
2. Explore **OpenCV (for AI in computer vision)** and **TensorRT (for deep learning acceleration)**.
3. Build projects integrating AI into games or robotics.

1.3 Rust – Secure AI for Edge Computing

Rust is gaining traction in AI development, especially for **edge computing** and **secure AI applications**.

+ **Memory Safety** – Prevents memory leaks and crashes, making AI models safer.
+ **Concurrency & Performance** – Ideal for AI in IoT devices and real-time systems.
+ **Efficient AI in low-power devices** – Perfect for deploying AI on embedded systems.

Example Use Case:

- AI-powered **smart cameras** that detect faces and objects in real-time using Rust-based ML models.
- **Embedded AI applications** in drones and robotics.

Getting Started with Rust for AI:

1. Learn Rust fundamentals (ownership, lifetimes, and safe concurrency).
2. Explore **tch-rs (Rust binding for PyTorch)** and **Rust Machine Learning (Rust ML)**.
3. Develop small AI models for IoT devices.

1.4 Julia – High-Performance AI for Scientific Computing

Julia is a **high-performance language** designed for numerical computing and AI in scientific applications.

+ **Faster than Python for AI calculations** – Great for simulations and large datasets.
+ **Optimized for Machine Learning** – Has AI-specific libraries like **Flux.jl** and **MLJ.jl**.
+ **Best for Scientific AI Applications** – Used in climate modeling, physics, and bioinformatics.

Example Use Case:

- AI-driven simulations for **weather forecasting**.
- **Financial modeling AI** for stock market predictions.

Getting Started with Julia for AI:

1. Install Julia and explore its package manager.

2. Learn **Flux.jl** for deep learning and **DifferentialEquations.jl** for AI simulations.
3. Work on AI projects that require fast numerical computations.

Takeways:

Mastering AI starts with choosing the right programming language. Python remains the **go-to language** for AI, but for performance-intensive applications, **C++ and Rust** are great choices. **Julia** is best for scientific AI, especially in research-based projects.

In the next chapter, we'll explore **essential AI frameworks** like TensorFlow, PyTorch, and Hugging Face, which will help you build, train, and deploy AI models effectively.

Key Takeaways from Chapter 1:
- **Python** – Best for general AI, deep learning, and AI agent development.
- **C++** – Ideal for real-time AI, gaming, and autonomous systems.
- **Rust** – Great for secure AI and edge computing.
- **Julia** – Best for high-performance AI in scientific computing.

Chapter 2: Machine Learning & Deep Learning Frameworks

Artificial Intelligence relies on **machine learning (ML) and deep learning (DL) frameworks** to train, optimize, and deploy models efficiently. These frameworks provide essential tools for **data processing, model training, and real-world AI applications**.

In this chapter, we will explore the most important ML and DL frameworks, their strengths, and how they are used in AI development.

2.1 TensorFlow – Google's AI Powerhouse

What is TensorFlow?
TensorFlow, developed by **Google Brain**, is one of the most powerful and widely used deep learning libraries. It provides **tools for building, training, and deploying AI models** across various platforms, from cloud servers to mobile devices.

+ **High Performance** – Uses GPUs and TPUs for accelerated computation.
+ **Scalable** – Ideal for both research and enterprise AI applications.
+ **End-to-End AI** – Supports deep learning, reinforcement learning, and large-scale AI systems.

+ **TensorFlow Lite** – Deploy AI models on mobile and edge devices.
+ **TensorFlow Extended (TFX)** – A complete pipeline for deploying AI in production.

Example Use Case:

- Training an **image recognition model** to detect objects in photos using **CNNs (Convolutional Neural Networks)**.
- Developing a **speech recognition AI** for transcribing spoken words into text.

Getting Started with TensorFlow:

1. Install TensorFlow:

   bash

   pip install tensorflow

2. Build a simple neural network:

   python

   ```python
   import tensorflow as tf
   from tensorflow import keras

   # Define a basic neural network
   model = keras.Sequential([
       keras.layers.Dense(64, activation='relu'),
       keras.layers.Dense(10, activation='softmax')
   ```

```
])

model.compile(optimizer='adam',
loss='categorical_crossentropy',
metrics=['accuracy'])
```

3. Train and test the model with real-world data.

Best for: Computer vision, speech processing, and large-scale AI applications.

2.2 PyTorch – The Researcher's Favorite

What is PyTorch?
PyTorch, developed by **Facebook AI Research (FAIR)**, is the **most popular deep learning framework among researchers**. It provides a **flexible, dynamic computation graph** that makes model experimentation easy.

+ **Dynamic Computation Graph** – Allows flexible model building and debugging.
+ **Strong Community Support** – Used by top AI researchers worldwide.
+ **Integration with Hugging Face** – Easy access to pre-trained NLP models.
+ **TorchScript & ONNX** – Deploy models efficiently in production.
+ **Great for GANs & NLP** – Used in text generation and AI art applications.

Example Use Case:

- Building a **Chatbot AI** using **Hugging Face's transformers**.
- Training a **GAN (Generative Adversarial Network)** to generate realistic images.

Getting Started with PyTorch:

1. Install PyTorch:

bash

pip install torch torchvision torchaudio

2. Build a simple neural network:

python

```
import torch
import torch.nn as nn

class NeuralNet(nn.Module):
    def __init__(self):
        super(NeuralNet, self).__init__()
        self.fc1 = nn.Linear(64, 10)

    def forward(self, x):
        return self.fc1(x)

model = NeuralNet()
```

3. Train the model using **backpropagation** and optimize with **Adam**.

Best for: Research, experimentation, NLP, and computer vision.

2.3 JAX – Google's High-Performance AI Engine

What is JAX?
JAX, developed by **Google DeepMind**, is an **alternative to PyTorch and TensorFlow** that focuses on high-performance **automatic differentiation and parallel computing**. It is particularly useful in **reinforcement learning and scientific AI applications**.

+ **Optimized for TPUs & GPUs** – Superfast training and inference.
+ **Autograd & XLA Compilation** – Highly efficient computation.
+ **Used by DeepMind** – Powers cutting-edge AI models like AlphaFold.
+ **Ideal for Reinforcement Learning** – Used in AI-driven decision-making models.

Example Use Case:

- **AlphaGo-style AI** for playing complex strategy games using **reinforcement learning**.

- **Physics simulations** that require high-speed mathematical calculations.

Getting Started with JAX:

1. Install JAX:

   bash

   pip install jax jaxlib

2. Define a function and use JAX's automatic differentiation:

   python

   ```
   import jax.numpy as jnp
   from jax import grad

   def loss_fn(x):
       return jnp.sum(x ** 2)

   grad_fn = grad(loss_fn)
   print(grad_fn(jnp.array([3.0, 4.0, 5.0])))
   ```

Best for: Reinforcement learning, scientific computing, and cutting-edge AI research.

2.4 Keras – Rapid Prototyping for Deep Learning

What is Keras?
Keras is a **high-level API for TensorFlow** that makes

deep learning more accessible. It allows developers to quickly build AI models **without writing complex low-level code**.

+ **Beginner-Friendly** – Simple API for AI development.
+ **Integrates with TensorFlow** – Uses TensorFlow as the backend.
+ **Great for Prototyping** – Ideal for quick experimentation.
+ **Pre-Trained Models** – Use Keras Applications for AI transfer learning.

Example Use Case:

- Developing an **image classifier** with **just a few lines of code**.
- Fine-tuning **pre-trained AI models** like MobileNet for object detection.

Getting Started with Keras:

1. Install Keras:

   bash

   pip install tensorflow

2. Build a deep learning model with Keras:

   python

   from tensorflow import keras

```
model = keras.Sequential([
    keras.layers.Dense(128, activation='relu'),
    keras.layers.Dense(10, activation='softmax')
])

model.compile(optimizer='adam',
loss='categorical_crossentropy',
metrics=['accuracy'])
```

Best for: Beginners, prototyping, and quick AI model development.

In conclusion, choosing the right ML/DL framework depends on **your experience level and project requirements**.

- **TensorFlow** – Best for large-scale AI and enterprise applications.
- **PyTorch** – Ideal for research and cutting-edge AI development.
- **JAX** – Optimized for high-performance AI, reinforcement learning, and scientific computing.
- **Keras** – The easiest way to prototype and build deep learning models quickly.

In the next chapter, we'll explore **AI development environments, cloud computing, and MLOps tools** to help you manage AI models in production.

Chapter 3: AI Agent & Reinforcement Learning (RL) Frameworks

Artificial Intelligence (AI) agents are at the heart of **autonomous decision-making systems**. From self-driving cars to gaming AI and robotic automation, reinforcement learning (RL) plays a crucial role in training AI agents.

In this chapter, we will explore the **top AI agent and reinforcement learning frameworks** that allow developers to train, test, and deploy AI agents in real-world and simulated environments.

3.1 Stable-Baselines3 (SB3) – The Go-To RL Framework for Training AI Agents

What is Stable-Baselines3?

Stable-Baselines3 (SB3) is a Python library for training **reinforcement learning (RL) agents** efficiently. It provides **pre-implemented state-of-the-art RL algorithms** and is widely used for AI applications in **robotics, gaming, finance, and automation**.

+ **Pre-Implemented RL Algorithms** – Includes **PPO, DQN, A2C, SAC, TD3**, and more.
+ **Easy to Use** – Built with a simple API for fast

experimentation.

+ **Works with Gym Environments** – Compatible with **OpenAI Gym** and **Gymnasium**.

+ **Multi-Agent Support** – Train multiple AI agents simultaneously.

+ **Supports TensorFlow & PyTorch** – Flexible model customization.

Example Use Cases:

- Training **autonomous robots** to navigate real-world environments.
- Developing **AI players** for board games and video games.
- Creating **algorithmic trading bots** that adapt to market conditions.

Getting Started with Stable-Baselines3:

1. **Install SB3**:
2. pip install stable-baselines3[extra]
3. **Train a Reinforcement Learning Agent in a Gym Environment**:
4. from stable_baselines3 import PPO
5. from gymnasium.envs.classic_control import CartPoleEnv
6.
7. # Create the environment
8. env = CartPoleEnv()
9.
10. # Define and train the agent

```
11.  model = PPO("MlpPolicy", env, verbose=1)
12.  model.learn(total_timesteps=10000)
13.
14.  # Test the trained AI agent
15.  obs = env.reset()
16.  for _ in range(1000):
17.      action, _states = model.predict(obs)
18.      obs, rewards, done, info = env.step(action)
19.      if done:
20.          obs = env.reset()
```

Best for: Autonomous robots, game AI, and intelligent control systems.

3.2 RLlib – Scalable Reinforcement Learning for Large-Scale AI Applications

What is RLlib?

RLlib is an advanced **scalable RL library** built on top of **Ray**, a framework designed for distributed computing. RLlib is used by major companies like **Uber, Google DeepMind, and OpenAI** for training **large-scale AI agents**.

+ **Distributed Training** – Trains AI agents across multiple GPUs/CPUs.
+ **Cloud Integration** – Works with AWS, GCP, and Azure for large-scale AI training.
+ **Multi-Agent Learning** – Supports training **multiple**

AI agents in the same environment.
+ **Supports All Major RL Algorithms** – Includes **PPO, DQN, SAC, IMPALA**, and more.
+ **Production-Ready** – Used in **self-driving cars, supply chain optimization, and robotics**.

Example Use Cases:

- **Autonomous vehicles** learning to drive in simulated environments.
- **Financial AI** optimizing stock trading strategies.
- **Healthcare AI** for personalized medical treatment recommendations.

Getting Started with RLlib:

1. **Install Ray & RLlib**:
2. pip install ray[rllib]
3. **Train an RL Agent in a Gym Environment**:
4. import ray
5. from ray.rllib.algorithms.ppo import PPO
6. from gymnasium.envs.classic_control import CartPoleEnv
7.
8. # Initialize Ray
9. ray.init()
10.
11. # Define the agent configuration
12. config = {
13.   "env": CartPoleEnv,
14.   "num_workers": 2, # Parallel training

```
15.    "framework": "torch",  # Can also use "tf"
16.  }
17.
18.  # Train the agent using PPO
19.  trainer = PPO(config=config)
20.  for i in range(10):
21.      results = trainer.train()
22.      print(f"Iteration {i}:
    {results['episode_reward_mean']}")
23.
24.  # Shut down Ray after training
25.  ray.shutdown()
```

Best for: Large-scale AI agent training, cloud-based reinforcement learning, and self-driving AI.

3.3 Gymnasium (OpenAI Gym v2) – The Standard RL Simulation Platform

What is Gymnasium?

Gymnasium (formerly OpenAI Gym) is the **gold standard** for training **reinforcement learning** models in **simulated environments**. It provides a variety of pre-built **AI training environments**, ranging from **robotics simulations to classic control problems**.

+ **Wide Range of AI Training Environments** – Includes **CartPole, LunarLander, Atari, and MuJoCo**.
+ **Compatible with RL Frameworks** – Works with

SB3, RLlib, PyTorch, and TensorFlow.

+ **Easy to Use** – Provides a simple API for training AI models.

+ **Supports Custom Environments** – Developers can create their own AI simulation worlds.

Example Use Cases:

- **Testing AI agents** in a **safe, controlled environment** before deploying them in the real world.
- Training **robotic arms** to complete tasks using reinforcement learning.
- Developing **AI-powered drones** for autonomous navigation.

Getting Started with Gymnasium:

1. **Install Gymnasium**:
2. pip install gymnasium[classic_control]
3. **Create and Interact with a Gym Environment**:
4. import gymnasium as gym
5.
6. # Create an environment
7. env = gym.make("CartPole-v1")
8.
9. # Reset the environment
10. obs = env.reset()
11.
12. # Simulate a random agent
13. for _ in range(1000):

```
14.     action = env.action_space.sample()  #
     Choose a random action
15.     obs, reward, done, info = env.step(action)
16.     if done:
17.         obs = env.reset()
```

Best for: AI simulations, reinforcement learning research, and AI-powered robotics.

3.4 Unity ML-Agents – AI Agent Training for Gaming & Simulation

What is Unity ML-Agents?

Unity ML-Agents is a **reinforcement learning toolkit** for training AI agents in **3D simulations and video game environments**.

+ **Game AI Development** – Train AI agents for **NPC behavior** and strategy games.
+ **Realistic 3D Simulations** – Train AI in **virtual worlds before real-world deployment**.
+ **Multi-Agent Training** – Simulate AI teamwork in cooperative environments.
+ **Supports PPO & SAC Algorithms** – Uses advanced reinforcement learning methods.

Example Use Cases:

- **Game development** – Creating **intelligent NPCs (Non-Player Characters)**.
- **Autonomous drones** – Training AI-powered drones in virtual landscapes.
- **AI for robotics** – Simulating **robot behavior** before real-world deployment.

Getting Started with Unity ML-Agents:

1. Install Unity and ML-Agents Toolkit.
2. Use Python API to train reinforcement learning agents.

Best for: Game AI, virtual simulations, and robotics research.

Key Takeaways from Chapter 3:

- **Stable-Baselines3 (SB3)** – Easy RL training for beginners and professionals.
- **RLlib** – Scalable RL for cloud-based AI applications.
- **Gymnasium** – The gold standard for AI agent testing.
- **Unity ML-Agents** – Best for game AI and 3D simulations.

Chapter 4: Large Language Models (LLMs) & NLP Tools

Large Language Models (LLMs) and Natural Language Processing (NLP) tools have revolutionized AI by enabling chatbots, AI agents, automated content generation, and intelligent search systems. Mastering LLMs is essential for building **conversational AI, text analysis applications, and AI-powered search engines**.

In this chapter, we'll cover the **most powerful tools and frameworks** used in LLM development, including **Hugging Face Transformers, LangChain, LlamaIndex, and SentenceTransformers**.

4.1 Hugging Face Transformers – The Core of LLM Development

What is Hugging Face Transformers?

Hugging Face provides a **library of pre-trained LLMs** like **GPT, LLaMA, Falcon, and Mistral**, which developers can fine-tune and deploy for AI applications. It is the **most widely used NLP framework**, enabling everything from chatbots to AI-powered summarization.

+ **Thousands of Pre-Trained Models** – Includes **GPT, BERT, LLaMA, Falcon, and Mistral**.
+ **Supports Multiple Frameworks** – Works with **PyTorch and TensorFlow**.
+ **Fine-Tuning & Customization** – Train models for **chatbots, search engines, and AI assistants**.
+ **Easy API Access** – Use models via API without complex setup.

Example Use Cases:

- **AI Chatbots** – Deploy conversational AI like ChatGPT.
- **Text Summarization** – Automatically condense large texts.
- **Machine Translation** – Translate languages using advanced AI.
- **AI Writing Assistants** – Generate high-quality AI-driven content.

Getting Started with Hugging Face Transformers:

1. **Install the Library**:

bash

pip install transformers

2. **Load a Pre-Trained GPT Model**:

python

```
from transformers import pipeline

generator = pipeline("text-generation",
model="gpt2")
response = generator("What is AI?",
max_length=50)
print(response)
```

Best for: AI chatbots, NLP research, content generation, and text analysis.

4.2 LangChain – The Framework for Building AI Agents with LLMs

What is LangChain?

LangChain is a powerful framework for building **LLM-powered applications** and AI agents. It allows developers to connect LLMs with **databases, APIs, and memory systems** to create **context-aware AI agents**.

+ **Enables AI Agents** – Create **memory-enhanced, multi-step AI workflows**.
+ **Connects to APIs & Databases** – Use external data sources with LLMs.
+ **Works with Multiple LLMs** – Supports **GPT, LLaMA, Falcon, and Mistral**.
+ **Ideal for Autonomous AI Systems** – Train AI agents for complex tasks.

Example Use Cases:

- **AI Customer Support Bots** – LLM-powered assistants for businesses.
- **Automated Research Assistants** – AI that searches and summarizes articles.
- **AI-Powered Coding Assistants** – AI agents that help developers debug code.

Getting Started with LangChain:

1. **Install LangChain**:

   bash

   pip install langchain

2. **Build an LLM-Powered AI Agent**:

   python

   ```
   from langchain.chat_models import ChatOpenAI
   from langchain.schema import AIMessage,
   HumanMessage

   chat_model = ChatOpenAI(model="gpt-4")
   response =
   chat_model([HumanMessage(content="How does
   AI work?")])
   print(response)
   ```

Best for: AI chatbots, automation, and intelligent AI assistants.

4.3 LlamaIndex – Connecting LLMs to External Knowledge Bases

What is LlamaIndex?

LlamaIndex (formerly GPT Index) helps **connect LLMs to databases, APIs, and document storage**. This makes it possible to build **AI-powered search engines and knowledge retrieval systems**.

+ **Enhances LLM Capabilities** – Connects AI models to structured data.
+ **Works with Any Database** – Supports **SQL, NoSQL, and vector databases**.
+ **Ideal for Enterprise AI** – Helps create **intelligent AI-driven search engines**.
+ **Compatible with LangChain** – Can be combined to create **powerful AI agents**.

Example Use Cases:

- **AI-Powered Search Systems** – Connect AI models to large document databases.
- **Enterprise Chatbots** – AI bots that retrieve company-specific knowledge.
- **Legal & Medical AI Assistants** – AI that provides context-aware legal/medical answers.

Getting Started with LlamaIndex:

1. **Install LlamaIndex**:

   bash

   pip install llama-index

2. **Load Documents & Query AI**:

   python

   ```python
   from llama_index import GPTVectorStoreIndex, SimpleDirectoryReader

   # Load documents
   documents = SimpleDirectoryReader("data/").load_data()

   # Build AI index
   index = GPTVectorStoreIndex.from_documents(documents)

   # Query AI
   query_engine = index.as_query_engine()
   response = query_engine.query("What is the history of AI?")
   print(response)
   ```

Best for: AI search engines, enterprise AI applications, and knowledge retrieval systems.

4.4 SentenceTransformers – Semantic Search & Text Embeddings

What is SentenceTransformers?

SentenceTransformers provides **advanced text embedding models** for **semantic search, similarity matching, and AI-powered text classification**.

+ **State-of-the-Art Text Embeddings** – Converts text into AI-readable vector representations.
+ **Enables AI-Powered Search** – Used in **Google-style AI search engines**.
+ **Ideal for AI Content Analysis** – Helps categorize and compare documents.
+ **Works with Hugging Face Transformers** – Integrates seamlessly with NLP models.

Example Use Cases:

- **AI-Powered Search Engines** – Build search tools that **understand meaning, not just keywords**.
- **Chatbot Memory Systems** – AI bots that recall **context from past conversations**.
- **AI-Powered Recommendation Systems** – Find **similar articles, products, or answers**.

Getting Started with SentenceTransformers:

1. **Install SentenceTransformers**:

bash

pip install sentence-transformers

2. **Generate AI-Powered Text Embeddings**:

python

from sentence_transformers import SentenceTransformer

model = SentenceTransformer("all-MiniLM-L6-v2")

sentences = ["Artificial intelligence is transforming industries.",
        "AI is changing the world."]

embeddings = model.encode(sentences)
print(embeddings)

 Best for: AI-powered search, chatbot memory, and intelligent recommendations.

Key Takeaways from Chapter 4:

- **Hugging Face Transformers** – The foundation for LLM development.

- **LangChain** – Enables AI agents with LLMs.
- **LlamaIndex** – Connects AI to external data sources.
- **SentenceTransformers** – Enables **semantic search & AI-powered recommendations**.

Chapter 5: AI Agents & Autonomous Systems

Artificial Intelligence (AI) agents and autonomous systems are at the forefront of AI development, enabling **self-improving, decision-making, and task-automating AI**. From **AutoGPT** to **BabyAGI**, and strategic AI like **Meta AI's CICERO**, these technologies push the boundaries of automation.

In this chapter, we'll cover:
+ **AI agents that automate workflows** (AutoGPT, BabyAGI)
+ **Self-learning AI in gaming** (Voyager)
+ **Strategic AI decision-making** (CICERO)
+ **Multi-agent collaboration AI** (AgentGPT, CrewAI)

5.1 AutoGPT & BabyAGI – Open-Source AI Agents for Automating Workflows

What are AutoGPT & BabyAGI?

AutoGPT and **BabyAGI** are open-source AI agents that **autonomously break down tasks, generate action plans, and execute them without human intervention**. They use LLMs (like GPT-4) to **analyze problems, make decisions, and complete goals** step by step.

+ **Automates Complex Tasks** – AI plans and executes workflows without human input.
+ **Uses LLMs & APIs** – Powered by **GPT-4, vector databases, and external APIs**.
+ **Self-Improving** – AI agents **learn and refine** their workflows.
+ **Multi-Step Reasoning** – Can complete projects requiring multiple steps.

Example Use Cases:

- **Automated Market Research** – AI searches the web, summarizes trends, and generates reports.
- **AI-Powered Coding Assistants** – AutoGPT writes and debugs code.
- **AI-Driven Business Automation** – Automates repetitive office workflows.

Getting Started with AutoGPT:

1. **Install AutoGPT:**
2. git clone https://github.com/Torantulino/Auto-GPT.git
3. cd Auto-GPT
4. pip install -r requirements.txt
5. **Run AutoGPT with Your API Key:**
6. python -m autogpt --api-key "YOUR_OPENAI_API_KEY"

Best for: AI-powered automation, research, and workflow optimization.

5.2 Voyager – Self-Improving AI in Open-World Environments (Minecraft AI Agent)

What is Voyager?

Voyager is an **autonomous, self-improving AI agent for open-world gaming environments**. It learns by **trial and error**, improving its capabilities over time. Unlike scripted AI, Voyager **adapts dynamically** to changing environments.

+ **Self-Learning AI** – Continuously improves through reinforcement learning.
+ **Understands Open-World Environments** – Adapts to challenges dynamically.
+ **Uses GPT for Decision-Making** – Generates plans & strategies in real-time.
+ **Optimized for Gaming AI** – Specifically designed for AI **learning in games**.

Example Use Cases:

- **Game AI Development** – Training AI for open-world games.
- **AI in Simulated Environments** – AI that **learns & adapts** over time.
- **Autonomous AI Agents** – Self-improving AI for robotics & automation.

Getting Started with Voyager:

1. **Install the Voyager AI Package**:

2. git clone
   https://github.com/MineDojo/Voyager.git
3. cd Voyager
4. pip install -r requirements.txt
5. **Run Voyager in Minecraft:**
6. python run.py --world "Minecraft"

 Best for: AI learning in **gaming, simulations, and adaptive AI research**.

5.3 Meta AI's CICERO – AI for Strategic Reasoning & Diplomacy

What is CICERO?

Meta AI's **CICERO** is a **strategic AI agent** built for complex **multi-agent interactions**. It excels in **long-term planning, negotiation, and diplomacy**, making it one of the most advanced AI agents for **human-like reasoning**.

+ **Understands Human Intentions** – Interprets & responds to human strategies.
+ **Plays Diplomacy at Superhuman Level** – Won competitive human games.
+ **Combines NLP with Reinforcement Learning** – Blends conversation & decision-making.
+ **Designed for Multi-Agent AI** – Used in **economic simulations & strategic AI**.

Example Use Cases:

- **AI-Powered Diplomacy & Strategy Games** – AI playing complex negotiation games.
- **Multi-Agent AI Training** – AI agents cooperating & competing in simulations.
- **Economic & Business AI Models** – AI for **strategic business planning**.

Getting Started with CICERO:

1. **Install Meta's AI Packages**
2. pip install fairseq
3. **Run CICERO AI Model**
4. from fairseq.models.transformer import TransformerModel
5. cicero = TransformerModel.from_pretrained("meta-cicero")
6. print(cicero.generate("How should I negotiate in diplomacy?"))

Best for: AI in strategy games, negotiations, and business planning AI.

5.4 AgentGPT & CrewAI – Open-Source Multi-Agent AI Frameworks

What is AgentGPT?

AgentGPT is a **multi-agent AI system** where multiple **AI agents collaborate** to complete tasks. It **breaks down complex projects** by assigning specialized AI sub-agents to handle different parts of the task.

+ **Multi-Agent AI Collaboration** – AI agents work together to complete objectives.
+ **Can Be Fine-Tuned** – Each agent can specialize in a different skill.
+ **Works with OpenAI's GPT Models** – Uses LLMs to power each agent.
+ **Designed for Task Automation** – Ideal for handling **large-scale AI workflows**.

Example Use Cases:

- **AI Project Managers** – AI agents assigning and overseeing tasks.
- **Automated Content Research & Writing** – Multi-agent teams researching & writing articles.
- **Enterprise AI Assistants** – AI agents managing office workflows.

Getting Started with AgentGPT:

1. **Install AgentGPT**
2. pip install agentgpt
3. **Run a Multi-Agent Workflow**
4. from agentgpt import Agent
5.

6. agent1 = Agent("Researcher", "Find top 10 AI trends for 2025")
7. agent2 = Agent("Writer", "Write an article based on Researcher's data")
8.
9. agent1.execute()
10. agent2.execute()

Best for: AI-driven workflow automation & multi-agent AI collaboration.

Key Takeaways from Chapter 5:

- **AutoGPT & BabyAGI** – AI automating complex tasks & workflows.
- **Voyager** – Self-learning AI in gaming & simulations.
- **Meta CICERO** – Strategic AI for negotiations & diplomacy.
- **AgentGPT & CrewAI** – AI agents collaborating to complete tasks.

Chapter 6: Data Processing & Engineering

In AI development, **high-quality data is the backbone** of every machine learning and AI model. **Data processing and engineering** ensure that raw data is cleaned, structured, and optimized for AI applications. Without efficient data pipelines, even the most powerful AI algorithms will fail to deliver reliable results.

This chapter covers:
+ **Essential tools for data manipulation** (Pandas, Dask)
+ **Big data processing frameworks** (Apache Spark)
+ **High-performance alternatives for AI-scale data processing** (Polars)

6.1 Pandas – The Essential Tool for Data Manipulation

What is Pandas?

Pandas is **the most widely used Python library** for handling structured data. It provides **powerful tools for data cleaning, transformation, and exploration**, making it essential for AI engineers and data scientists.

+ **Easy-to-use API** – Simplifies data analysis and transformation.

+ **Supports CSV, Excel, JSON, SQL, and more** – Works with multiple data formats.

+ **Built-in handling of missing data** – Automates data cleaning.

+ **Ideal for small to medium-sized datasets** – Optimized for tabular data.

Example Use Cases:

- **Preprocessing AI training data** – Cleaning and structuring datasets for ML models.
- **Exploratory Data Analysis (EDA)** – Identifying trends and insights.
- **Feature Engineering** – Extracting relevant features for AI models.

Getting Started with Pandas:

1. **Install Pandas**

   bash

   pip install pandas

2. **Load a Dataset**

   python

   import pandas as pd

```
df = pd.read_csv("data.csv")
print(df.head())  # Display first 5 rows
```

Best for: Data preprocessing, cleaning, and small-to-medium dataset analysis.

6.2 Dask – Scalable Data Processing for AI Pipelines

What is Dask?

Dask is an **advanced data processing framework that extends Pandas for large-scale datasets**. It enables parallel computing, allowing AI developers to process massive amounts of data **without running into memory limitations**.

+ **Works like Pandas** – Easy transition from Pandas to Dask.
+ **Handles datasets too large for RAM** – Uses parallel computing and out-of-core execution.
+ **Optimized for AI model training** – Speeds up feature engineering.
+ **Works with Jupyter Notebooks & Cloud Computing** – Ideal for large-scale AI projects.

Example Use Cases:

- **Processing big data for AI training** – Handles datasets larger than memory.

- **Parallel computing in AI pipelines** – Speeds up feature extraction and transformations.
- **Distributed computing in cloud AI models** – Scales across multiple CPU cores.

Getting Started with Dask:

1. **Install Dask**

   bash

   pip install dask

2. **Process a Large Dataset**

   python

   import dask.dataframe as dd

   ```
   df = dd.read_csv("large_dataset.csv")
   print(df.head())  # Lazy computation, processes
   data in parallel
   ```

Best for: Large-scale AI datasets, parallel data processing, and cloud-based AI applications.

6.3 Apache Spark – Big Data Processing for AI Pipelines

What is Apache Spark?

Apache Spark is **the leading big data processing framework**, used for handling petabyte-scale datasets. It is widely used in AI applications that **require distributed computing across multiple nodes**.

+ **In-memory processing** – Faster than Hadoop for big data.
+ **Works with ML and AI frameworks** – Supports PySpark, MLlib, and TensorFlow.
+ **Handles structured & unstructured data** – Works with CSV, JSON, Parquet, and databases.
+ **Optimized for real-time AI applications** – Used in fraud detection, recommendation systems, and IoT AI.

Example Use Cases:

- **Training AI models on massive datasets** – Used in Google, Netflix, and Facebook AI pipelines.
- **Real-time AI processing** – AI applications in banking, security, and IoT.
- **Big data analytics for AI** – Extracting insights from large-scale data.

Getting Started with Apache Spark:

1. **Install PySpark**

bash

```
pip install pyspark
```

2. **Process Big Data in Spark**

python

```
from pyspark.sql import SparkSession

spark = SparkSession.builder.appName("AIDataProcessing").getOrCreate()
df = spark.read.csv("bigdata.csv", header=True, inferSchema=True)
df.show()  # Displays the first few rows
```

Best for: Large-scale AI model training, big data analytics, and real-time AI applications.

6.4 Polars – Faster Alternative to Pandas for AI Data Processing

What is Polars?

Polars is a **high-performance data manipulation library** designed for AI and machine learning workloads. It is a **faster alternative to Pandas**, optimized for large datasets.

+ **10-100x faster than Pandas** – Built on Rust for performance.
+ **Multi-threaded processing** – Uses all CPU cores for faster computations.
+ **Handles large datasets efficiently** – Ideal for AI and big data.
+ **Compatible with Pandas syntax** – Easy transition from Pandas.

Example Use Cases:

- **Processing AI datasets at scale** – Faster AI data handling.
- **Speeding up ML pipelines** – Optimized for feature extraction.
- **Replacing Pandas for performance-intensive tasks** – Ideal for AI engineers working with big data.

Getting Started with Polars:

1. **Install Polars**

   bash

   pip install polars

2. **Load & Process Data with Polars**

   python

```
import polars as pl

df = pl.read_csv("large_data.csv")
print(df.head())  # Displays the first few rows
efficiently
```

Best for: AI engineers needing **high-speed, scalable data processing**.

Key Takeaways from Chapter 6:

- **Pandas** – Best for small-to-medium AI datasets and data exploration.
- **Dask** – Best for scaling Pandas workflows for big AI datasets.
- **Apache Spark** – Best for large-scale AI processing and distributed computing.
- **Polars** – Best for high-performance AI data manipulation.

Chapter 7: Computer Vision (CV) Tools

Computer vision (CV) is a **core AI discipline** that enables machines to interpret and process images and videos. From facial recognition to self-driving cars and medical imaging, **CV powers some of the most groundbreaking AI applications today**.

This chapter covers:
+ **Essential libraries for image processing** (OpenCV)
+ **Advanced object detection models** (Detectron2, YOLO)
+ **State-of-the-art segmentation models** (Segment Anything Model - SAM)

7.1 OpenCV – The Foundation of Computer Vision

What is OpenCV?

OpenCV (Open Source Computer Vision Library) is **the most widely used library for image processing and computer vision tasks**. It provides powerful tools to **manipulate, enhance, and analyze images/videos**, making it essential for AI developers.

+ **Supports multiple languages** – Works with Python, C++, and Java.
+ **Real-time image & video processing** – Used in robotics, surveillance, and AR.

+ **Pre-built algorithms** – Includes face detection, object tracking, and edge detection.
+ **Works with deep learning** – Compatible with TensorFlow, PyTorch, and ONNX.

Example Use Cases:

- **Preprocessing images for AI models** – Normalization, resizing, and filtering.
- **Facial recognition and motion detection** – Used in security systems.
- **Medical imaging analysis** – Enhancing X-rays, MRIs, and CT scans.

Getting Started with OpenCV:

1. **Install OpenCV**
2. pip install opencv-python
3. **Load and Display an Image**
4. import cv2
5.
6. img = cv2.imread("image.jpg")
7. cv2.imshow("Image", img)
8. cv2.waitKey(0)
9. cv2.destroyAllWindows()

Best for: Image preprocessing, feature extraction, and real-time vision applications.

7.2 Detectron2 – Facebook's Object Detection Framework

What is Detectron2?

Developed by Meta AI (formerly Facebook AI), Detectron2 is a **state-of-the-art object detection and instance segmentation framework** built on PyTorch. It powers advanced AI models that can **detect, classify, and segment objects in real time**.

+ **Pre-trained deep learning models** – Faster R-CNN, Mask R-CNN, RetinaNet.
+ **High accuracy object detection** – Used in AI-powered surveillance and automation.
+ **Built-in training pipeline** – Fine-tune models with custom datasets.
+ **Scalable & efficient** – Optimized for large-scale AI applications.

Example Use Cases:

- **Autonomous vehicles** – Real-time object detection for self-driving cars.
- **Retail & security** – Automated checkout systems, face detection in CCTV.
- **Medical AI** – Detecting anomalies in medical scans (X-rays, MRIs).

Getting Started with Detectron2:

1. **Install Detectron2**

2. pip install
'git+https://github.com/facebookresearch/detectron2.git'
3. **Run Object Detection on an Image**
4. import torch
5. import detectron2
6. from detectron2.engine import DefaultPredictor
7. from detectron2.config import get_cfg
8. from detectron2.utils.visualizer import Visualizer
9. import cv2
10.
11. cfg = get_cfg()
12. cfg.merge_from_file("detectron2/configs/COCO-
    InstanceSegmentation/mask_rcnn_R_50_FPN_3x.yaml")
13. cfg.MODEL.WEIGHTS = "model_final.pth" # Load pre-trained model
14. predictor = DefaultPredictor(cfg)
15.
16. img = cv2.imread("test.jpg")
17. outputs = predictor(img)
18.
19. v = Visualizer(img[:, :, ::-1])
20. out = v.draw_instance_predictions(outputs["instances"].to("cpu"))
21. cv2.imshow("Detected Objects", out.get_image()[:, :, ::-1])
22. cv2.waitKey(0)

Best for: AI-powered security, medical imaging, and autonomous systems.

7.3 YOLO (You Only Look Once) – Real-Time Object Detection

What is YOLO?

YOLO (You Only Look Once) is **the fastest object detection model**, widely used in **real-time applications** like robotics, surveillance, and self-driving cars. Unlike traditional object detection models, YOLO **detects all objects in a single pass**, making it **extremely efficient**.

+ **Ultra-fast object detection** – 30-60 FPS, ideal for real-time AI.
+ **Trained on COCO dataset** – Can detect 80+ objects out-of-the-box.
+ **Lightweight & scalable** – Works on edge devices (Jetson Nano, Raspberry Pi).
+ **Great for AI automation** – Used in drones, robotics, and video analytics.

Example Use Cases:

- **Self-driving cars** – Detecting pedestrians, vehicles, and road signs.
- **AI-powered surveillance** – Real-time threat detection.

- **Retail automation** – AI-assisted checkout and inventory tracking.

Getting Started with YOLO:

1. **Install YOLOv8**
2. pip install ultralytics
3. **Run YOLO Object Detection**
4. from ultralytics import YOLO
5.
6. model = YOLO("yolov8n.pt") # Load pre-trained YOLO model
7. results = model("image.jpg") # Detect objects in an image
8. results.show() # Display detected objects

Best for: Real-time AI applications, security, and robotics.

7.4 Segment Anything Model (SAM) – Meta AI's Advanced Segmentation Model

What is SAM?

SAM (Segment Anything Model) is **a revolutionary AI model from Meta** that can **automatically segment any object in an image or video with high precision**. Unlike traditional segmentation models, **SAM does not require training on specific objects—** it can **segment any object, even if it has never seen it before**.

+ **Zero-shot segmentation** – Works on unseen objects.
+ **High accuracy & flexibility** – Works across multiple domains (medical imaging, AR/VR).
+ **Fast inference time** – Optimized for real-time applications.
+ **Integration with AI agents** – Can enhance robotic vision systems.

Example Use Cases:

- **Medical AI** – Automated tumor and organ segmentation in X-rays.
- **Augmented Reality (AR)** – Object segmentation for interactive experiences.
- **AI-assisted content creation** – Automatic background removal for videos/images.

Getting Started with SAM:

1. **Install SAM**
2. pip install segment-anything
3. **Run Object Segmentation**
4. from segment_anything import sam_model_registry, SamPredictor
5.
6. model = sam_model_registry["vit_h"](checkpoint="sam_vit_h.pth")
7. predictor = SamPredictor(model)
8.
9. predictor.set_image("image.jpg")
10. mask = predictor.predict() # Generate segmentation mask

Best for: Advanced segmentation, medical imaging, AR/VR, and AI-powered editing tools.

Key Takeaways from Chapter 7:

- **OpenCV** – Best for image preprocessing and real-time vision applications.
- **Detectron2** – Best for object detection and instance segmentation.
- **YOLO** – Best for ultra-fast, real-time object detection.
- **SAM** – Best for advanced AI-powered segmentation.

Chapter 8: Speech & Audio AI

Speech and audio AI technologies enable machines to **understand, process, and generate human speech**. These tools are essential for **voice assistants, transcription services, real-time translation, and AI-generated speech**.

In this chapter, we cover:
+ **Speech recognition (ASR)** – Converting speech to text (Whisper, DeepSpeech).
+ **Text-to-speech (TTS)** – Generating human-like speech (Coqui TTS).
+ **Use cases & real-world applications** – AI-powered voice assistants, subtitles, and accessibility tools.

8.1 OpenAI Whisper – State-of-the-Art Speech Recognition (ASR)

What is Whisper?

Whisper is an **automatic speech recognition (ASR) model** developed by OpenAI. It can **transcribe and translate spoken language with high accuracy**, even in noisy environments.

+ **Supports multiple languages** – Transcribes & translates 50+ languages.

+ Handles accents & background noise – Trained on diverse real-world audio.

+ Fast & accurate – Can be used for live transcription and subtitles.

+ Great for AI-powered applications – Voice assistants, call centers, accessibility tools.

Example Use Cases:

- **Automated transcription** – Converting podcasts, interviews, and lectures into text.
- **Live captioning** – Real-time subtitles for online meetings.
- **Multilingual translation** – Converting spoken language into different texts.

Getting Started with Whisper:

1. **Install Whisper**
2. pip install openai-whisper
3. **Transcribe an Audio File**
4. import whisper
5.
6. model = whisper.load_model("base")
7. result = model.transcribe("audio.mp3")
8. print(result["text"])

Best for: Transcription, translation, and voice-driven AI applications.

8.2 Mozilla DeepSpeech – Open-Source Speech-to-Text AI

What is DeepSpeech?

Developed by Mozilla, DeepSpeech is **a fully open-source speech-to-text model** based on deep learning. It is optimized for **offline voice processing**, making it a great choice for **privacy-focused applications**.

+ **Lightweight & offline-capable** – Runs locally without internet.
+ **Trained on diverse datasets** – Works well with various accents and speech styles.
+ **Can be fine-tuned** – Customizable for different languages or industries.
+ **Good alternative to cloud-based ASR** – No need for API usage or cloud fees.

Example Use Cases:

- **Offline voice assistants** – AI-powered assistants without cloud dependency.
- **Privacy-focused speech AI** – Secure, offline transcription for confidential data.
- **Speech-driven accessibility tools** – Helping people with disabilities interact with computers.

Getting Started with DeepSpeech:

1. **Install DeepSpeech**
2. pip install deepspeech
3. **Run Speech-to-Text Transcription**

```
4.  import deepspeech
5.  import wave
6.  import numpy as np
7.
8.  model_file = "deepspeech-model.pbmm"
9.  model = deepspeech.Model(model_file)
10.
11. with wave.open("speech.wav", "rb") as audio:
12.     frames =
        np.frombuffer(audio.readframes(audio.getnframe
        s()), np.int16)
13.
14. text = model.stt(frames)
15. print(text)
```

Best for: Privacy-first AI applications, offline transcription, and customizable speech AI.

8.3 Coqui TTS – Open-Source Text-to-Speech (TTS) Model

What is Coqui TTS?

Coqui TTS is **a powerful open-source text-to-speech (TTS) model** that generates **natural, human-like speech**. Unlike commercial TTS services (Google, Amazon, Azure), **Coqui runs locally**, allowing developers to create custom AI voices without API fees.

+ **High-quality speech synthesis** – Generates realistic AI voices.

+ **Supports multiple languages** – Train and fine-tune models for different accents.

+ **Custom voice training** – Developers can create personalized AI voices.

+ **Fully open-source** – No restrictions on usage.

Example Use Cases:

- **AI-generated voiceovers** – Creating human-like narration for videos and audiobooks.
- **Personalized AI voices** – Custom speech models for virtual assistants.
- **Accessibility tools** – Helping visually impaired users with AI-generated speech.

Getting Started with Coqui TTS:

1. **Install Coqui TTS**
2. pip install TTS
3. **Convert Text to Speech**
4. from TTS.api import TTS
5.
6. tts = TTS("tts_models/en/ljspeech/tacotron2-DCA")
7. tts.tts_to_file(text="Hello, this is an AI-generated voice!", file_path="output.wav")

Best for: AI voice assistants, synthetic voice generation, and offline text-to-speech applications.

Key Takeaways from Chapter 8:

- **Whisper** – Best for multilingual speech-to-text AI with high accuracy.
- **DeepSpeech** – Best for offline, privacy-focused transcription.
- **Coqui TTS** – Best for AI-powered voice synthesis with customizable voices.

Chapter 9: AI Deployment & MLOps

AI deployment and MLOps (Machine Learning Operations) are essential components of the AI lifecycle, allowing you to transition machine learning models from development to production smoothly, efficiently, and at scale. This chapter will dive into the tools and technologies necessary for deploying AI models, managing their lifecycle, and optimizing their performance in production environments. Specifically, we'll cover Docker, Kubernetes (K8s), MLflow, and TensorRT, which are critical tools in modern AI and MLOps workflows.

---

1. Docker: Containerization for AI Applications

Docker is a powerful tool that enables you to package your application (including the environment, dependencies, and libraries) into containers. A container is a lightweight, standalone, and executable software package that includes everything needed to run an application, ensuring consistency across various environments.

Why Docker?

- **Portability:** Docker containers encapsulate an AI model and its dependencies, ensuring it runs the same way in development, testing, and production environments.

- **Isolation:** Containers provide an isolated environment, ensuring that dependencies and configurations do not conflict with the host system or other containers.
- **Scalability:** Containers allow for easy scaling of applications, making it easier to deploy AI models across multiple systems or cloud environments.

Key Concepts:

- **Docker Images:** These are read-only templates used to create containers. You can think of an image as a snapshot of a file system with all the necessary libraries and configurations to run your AI model.
- **Docker Containers:** These are running instances of Docker images, representing a live, executable environment for your AI model.
- **Dockerfile:** A script that contains a series of instructions to build a Docker image. It specifies the base image, dependencies, environment variables, and other configurations needed to run the AI model.

Example:

```
# Start with a base image that has Python installed
FROM python:3.8-slim
```

```
# Install dependencies (e.g., TensorFlow, PyTorch)
RUN pip install tensorflow pandas numpy scikit-learn

# Add the AI model code to the container
COPY my_model.py /app/

# Define the working directory inside the container
WORKDIR /app

# Set the entry point for running the model
CMD ["python", "my_model.py"]
```

By using Docker, you ensure that your AI model and its environment are consistent, enabling seamless deployment and scaling across different systems.

---

2. Kubernetes (K8s): Orchestrating AI Models in Production

Once you have containerized your AI models, managing their deployment and scaling efficiently becomes crucial. **Kubernetes (K8s)** is an open-source platform designed for automating the deployment, scaling, and operation of containerized applications. It orchestrates the deployment and management of Docker containers at scale, making it a fundamental tool for MLOps.

Why Kubernetes?

- **Scalability:** Kubernetes automates the scaling of AI models by managing multiple container replicas and distributing the load effectively.
- **Self-healing:** Kubernetes automatically monitors the health of AI models and replaces failed instances, ensuring that production systems remain up and running.
- **Load Balancing:** Kubernetes can balance requests across multiple instances of your AI model, ensuring optimal utilization of resources.
- **Distributed AI:** Kubernetes can efficiently manage distributed AI models, handling parallel processing and coordination between multiple services and containers.

Key Concepts:

- **Pods:** The smallest deployable units in Kubernetes, which encapsulate one or more containers. In the context of AI, a pod could represent a single instance of an AI model.
- **Deployments:** Kubernetes manages the desired state of an application using Deployments, ensuring that a specified number of replicas of an AI model are running at all times.
- **Services:** Kubernetes services expose the deployed AI model to the network, allowing clients to access the model through a stable IP address or DNS name.

- **Helm:** A Kubernetes package manager that simplifies the deployment and management of applications, including AI models.

Example:

```
apiVersion: apps/v1
kind: Deployment
metadata:
  name: ai-model-deployment
spec:
  replicas: 3
  selector:
    matchLabels:
      app: ai-model
  template:
    metadata:
      labels:
        app: ai-model
    spec:
      containers:
        - name: ai-model-container
          image: ai-model:latest
          ports:
            - containerPort: 8080
---
apiVersion: v1
kind: Service
metadata:
  name: ai-model-service
spec:
```

```
selector:
  app: ai-model
ports:
  - protocol: TCP
    port: 80
    targetPort: 8080
type: LoadBalancer
```

Kubernetes provides the ability to scale your AI models and manage them with minimal effort, making it a crucial tool for high-availability, production-grade AI systems.

---

3. MLflow: Tracking, Packaging, and Deploying AI Models

MLflow is an open-source platform designed to manage the machine learning lifecycle, including experimentation, reproducibility, and deployment. It allows you to track experiments, package code into reproducible runs, and deploy AI models efficiently.

Why MLflow?

- **Experiment Tracking:** MLflow enables you to track and log various machine learning experiments, such as model parameters, metrics, and artifacts, in a centralized repository.

- **Model Versioning:** MLflow facilitates versioning of AI models, making it easier to compare different versions of models and roll back to previous versions if necessary.
- **Model Deployment:** MLflow offers integrated tools to deploy models to cloud services, Kubernetes, or on-premises environments.
- **Reproducibility:** MLflow ensures that you can reproduce experiments with the exact same parameters, data, and environment, facilitating collaboration and debugging.

Key Concepts:

- **MLflow Tracking:** A component for logging and querying experiments, helping you track the performance of different models and configurations.
- **MLflow Projects:** Defines the structure of a machine learning project, including code, data, and environment dependencies.
- **MLflow Models:** A way to package AI models for deployment. MLflow supports multiple frameworks (e.g., TensorFlow, PyTorch) and can serve models through REST APIs or export them for use in production systems.
- **MLflow Registry:** A centralized repository for storing, versioning, and managing AI models in a collaborative environment.

Example:

```
import mlflow
import mlflow.tensorflow

# Log an experiment
with mlflow.start_run():
    model = train_model()  # Your AI model training
code
    mlflow.tensorflow.log_model(model, "model")

# Register the model for future use
mlflow.register_model("models:/model-
name/production", "path/to/your/model")
```

MLflow helps manage your AI models throughout their lifecycle, from experimentation and development to deployment, ensuring that models can be easily tracked, deployed, and updated.

---

4. TensorRT: NVIDIA's Optimization Framework for AI Inference

TensorRT is an NVIDIA deep learning optimization toolkit designed to optimize AI models for inference, particularly on NVIDIA GPUs. It enhances the performance of AI models by applying a variety of optimization techniques, such as precision calibration, layer fusion, and kernel auto-tuning, to achieve faster and more efficient inference.

Why TensorRT?

- **Performance Optimization:** TensorRT optimizes AI models for faster inference, enabling low-latency, high-throughput AI applications.
- **Hardware Acceleration:** TensorRT leverages the full potential of NVIDIA GPUs, providing hardware-accelerated AI inference.
- **Support for Multiple Frameworks:** TensorRT can optimize models trained in popular deep learning frameworks like TensorFlow, PyTorch, and ONNX.

Key Concepts:

- **FP16 and INT8 Precision:** TensorRT supports mixed-precision techniques like FP16 (16-bit floating point) and INT8 (8-bit integer) to accelerate inference without compromising accuracy.
- **Optimized Kernels:** TensorRT uses highly optimized kernels for NVIDIA GPUs, ensuring maximum efficiency during inference.
- **Dynamic Tensor Memory:** TensorRT can dynamically allocate and manage memory for AI models, optimizing the memory usage during inference.

Example:

```
import tensorrt as trt

# Load the trained model (in ONNX format)
onnx_model = 'model.onnx'
builder = trt.Builder(trt_logger)
network = builder.create_network()

# Parse the ONNX model into the TensorRT network
onnx_parser = trt.OnnxParser(network, trt_logger)
with open(onnx_model, 'rb') as f:
    onnx_parser.parse(f.read())

# Build the TensorRT engine
engine = builder.build_cuda_engine(network)
```

TensorRT significantly reduces inference time and increases throughput for AI models, making it an essential tool for deploying models in performance-critical applications.

In this chapter, we explored the core technologies necessary for successful AI deployment and MLOps: Docker for containerization, Kubernetes for orchestration, MLflow for lifecycle management, and TensorRT for optimization. Mastering these tools will enable you to manage and scale your AI models effectively, ensuring that they perform optimally in production environments. By leveraging these technologies, you can ensure smooth deployment, continuous monitoring, and high performance for your AI-powered applications.

Chapter 10: Edge AI & Embedded AI

Edge AI and Embedded AI are revolutionizing how we deploy and use artificial intelligence by pushing the capabilities of AI closer to the source of data generation. Instead of relying solely on cloud-based systems, AI models are being embedded in devices at the edge of networks, such as robotics, drones, and IoT devices. This chapter will explore key technologies in Edge AI, focusing on **NVIDIA Jetson**, **Google Coral**, and **Edge Impulse**, and their applications in embedded systems and edge devices.

---

1. NVIDIA Jetson: AI on Edge Devices (Robotics, Drones)

NVIDIA Jetson is a series of embedded computing boards that bring powerful AI computing to edge devices like robotics, drones, and autonomous machines. These boards integrate NVIDIA's powerful GPUs, enabling real-time AI processing directly on the device, without needing to send data back to the cloud. The Jetson platform is designed for edge computing and robotics, supporting computer vision, deep learning, and other AI-intensive tasks.

Why NVIDIA Jetson?

- **GPU-Powered AI:** Jetson boards are equipped with powerful GPUs, specifically designed to accelerate deep learning, computer vision, and AI inference tasks, allowing for real-time processing at the edge.
- **Low Power Consumption:** Despite their powerful capabilities, NVIDIA Jetson boards are optimized for low power consumption, making them ideal for embedded systems and mobile devices.
- **Wide Application Range:** Jetson can be used in various industries, from robotics and drones to industrial automation and smart cities, where real-time processing is critical.

Key Features:

- **CUDA and TensorRT Support:** Jetson supports NVIDIA's CUDA and TensorRT frameworks, ensuring efficient use of GPU resources for AI and deep learning tasks.
- **Comprehensive Ecosystem:** Jetson offers a robust ecosystem of software tools, libraries, and pre-trained models for deploying AI on edge devices, making it easier to develop and deploy AI applications.
- **Connectivity and Sensors:** The platform supports multiple I/O interfaces, including cameras, sensors, and networking ports,

allowing for seamless integration into complex edge systems like drones and robots.

Example: Jetson is commonly used in autonomous drones that process sensor data (such as camera feeds) locally to navigate obstacles or identify objects. This local processing allows drones to react in real-time without the latency introduced by sending data to the cloud for analysis.

Jetson Model Example:

```
# Setup for object detection on NVIDIA Jetson using TensorRT
sudo apt install python3-pip
pip3 install jetson-stats
# Deploy a pre-trained model for object detection
python3 detect_objects.py --model yolov5 --input /dev/video0
```

By leveraging NVIDIA Jetson, AI applications can run efficiently on edge devices with real-time processing, enabling autonomous systems that can operate without constant connectivity to the cloud.

---

2. Google Coral: AI Acceleration on Mobile/Embedded Systems

Google Coral is a suite of hardware and software products designed for deploying machine learning models on edge devices. Coral includes accelerators like the **Edge TPU** (Tensor Processing Unit), which provides high-speed AI inference with low power consumption, making it suitable for a wide range of embedded systems and mobile applications.

Why Google Coral?

- **AI at the Edge:** Coral allows machine learning models to run efficiently on edge devices, such as cameras, sensors, and mobile devices, without needing a cloud connection.
- **Edge TPU:** The Edge TPU is a purpose-built ASIC (Application-Specific Integrated Circuit) that accelerates tensor computations, providing a significant speedup for running AI models, especially for vision-related tasks.
- **Compact Form Factor:** Coral products come in small, low-power devices, making them ideal for resource-constrained environments such as IoT devices, wearables, and mobile applications.

Key Features:

- **TensorFlow Lite Compatibility:** Coral is tightly integrated with **TensorFlow Lite**, a lightweight version of TensorFlow, optimized for running on mobile and embedded devices with limited resources.
- **Real-Time Processing:** The Edge TPU allows Coral devices to process data in real-time,

making it suitable for applications such as object detection, facial recognition, and speech recognition directly on the device.

- **Low Power Consumption:** Coral devices are designed to run machine learning models with minimal power, which is essential for battery-operated IoT devices and mobile systems.

Example: Google Coral is often used in smart cameras that run object detection models directly on the device. These cameras can detect people or objects in real-time and trigger events like sending notifications, without sending data to the cloud.

Coral Example Code:

```
# Set up Coral with TensorFlow Lite model
pip3 install tensorflow
# Load a pre-trained model and run inference on
Coral's Edge TPU
python3 classify_image.py --model
mobilenet_v1_1.0_224_quant.tflite --device
/dev/apex_0
```

By leveraging Coral, embedded AI devices can perform powerful machine learning tasks with low latency, enabling efficient and intelligent systems at the edge.

3. Edge Impulse: ML Framework for Microcontrollers and IoT Devices

Edge Impulse is a platform designed to make machine learning accessible to developers working with microcontrollers and embedded devices. It provides a complete development environment for creating AI applications, from data collection and model training to deployment on small devices such as microcontrollers, IoT sensors, and wearables.

Why Edge Impulse?

- **Optimized for Small Devices:** Edge Impulse focuses on making machine learning feasible on resource-constrained devices like microcontrollers, which have limited processing power, memory, and storage.
- **End-to-End Workflow:** Edge Impulse provides an end-to-end workflow for building machine learning models, from collecting sensor data to training and deploying models, all within a unified platform.
- **Support for Various Hardware:** Edge Impulse supports a wide range of hardware platforms, including popular microcontrollers and development boards such as the Arduino Nano 33 BLE Sense, STMicroelectronics, and Raspberry Pi.

Key Features:

- **Sensor Data Integration:** Edge Impulse allows users to easily integrate sensor data from a variety of devices (e.g., accelerometers, gyros, cameras) and use it to train machine learning models.
- **Edge-Optimized Models:** The platform automatically optimizes models for edge devices, compressing and quantizing models to fit within the constraints of embedded systems.
- **Cloud and On-Device Inference:** Edge Impulse supports both cloud-based training and on-device inference, providing flexibility depending on the resource requirements and constraints of the target device.

Example: Edge Impulse is often used in wearable devices, such as fitness trackers, to analyze sensor data (e.g., heart rate, motion) and provide real-time feedback on the user's health status. These applications can run entirely on the device, reducing the need for cloud connectivity.

Edge Impulse Example Code:

```
# Install Edge Impulse CLI
npm install -g edge-impulse-cli
```

```
# Connect to the Edge Impulse platform and deploy a
model to an embedded device
edge-impulse-daemon --device /dev/ttyACM0
```

With Edge Impulse, developers can easily build and deploy machine learning models for embedded systems, democratizing access to AI for microcontroller-based applications.

Conclusion

Edge AI and Embedded AI bring the power of machine learning to devices that operate at the edge of the network, enabling real-time, efficient processing in environments with limited resources. **NVIDIA Jetson** offers powerful GPU acceleration for AI tasks in robotics and drones, while **Google Coral** provides AI acceleration through its Edge TPU for mobile and embedded systems. **Edge Impulse** enables developers to bring machine learning to microcontrollers and IoT devices, opening the door to AI-powered applications in small, low-power devices. By leveraging these tools, developers can create intelligent edge devices that process data locally, reducing latency, bandwidth usage, and reliance on the cloud.

Chapter 11: Synthetic Data & AI Simulation

In the rapidly advancing field of AI, data is king. However, acquiring large, high-quality datasets can be expensive, time-consuming, or even impractical in many situations. This is where **synthetic data** and **AI simulation** come into play. By generating artificial data or simulating environments, AI models can be trained without relying on real-world data. This chapter will explore some key tools and techniques for synthetic data generation and AI simulation, including **Unity Perception**, **Generative Adversarial Networks (GANs)**, and **DeepMind MuJoCo**.

---

1. Unity Perception: Generate Synthetic Data for AI Training

Unity Perception is a tool developed by Unity Technologies to generate synthetic data for training machine learning models. It is particularly useful in scenarios where collecting real-world data is difficult or too costly, such as in autonomous vehicle testing, robotics, or computer vision applications.

Why Unity Perception?

- **Realistic Environments:** Unity, a widely-used game development engine, provides highly realistic 3D environments for training AI models. These environments can include varied lighting conditions, weather effects, and dynamic object interactions.
- **Customizable Scenarios:** Unity Perception allows developers to create custom environments tailored to specific use cases, such as generating images of objects under different poses, angles, and lighting conditions, which are critical for training AI models like object detection and segmentation.
- **Data Augmentation:** It also supports generating massive amounts of labeled data by varying camera positions, lighting, and object configurations, leading to high-quality datasets for supervised learning tasks.

Key Features:

- **Multi-sensor Support:** Unity Perception can simulate data from multiple sensors, including cameras, LIDAR, and depth sensors, providing rich datasets for tasks such as object recognition and tracking.

- **Real-time Labeling:** Data can be automatically labeled in real-time during the simulation, saving time and effort in the manual annotation process.
- **Scalability:** Unity's powerful engine allows for the generation of large datasets in a fraction of the time it would take to collect data in the real world.

Example: Autonomous vehicle companies often use Unity Perception to generate synthetic driving data, training their AI models on how to detect and respond to various traffic situations, obstacles, and pedestrians under diverse conditions.

Unity Perception Example Code:

```
// Initialize the Perception Camera
using UnityEngine.Perception;

public class SyntheticDataGeneration :
MonoBehaviour
{
   void Start()
   {
     PerceptionCamera perceptionCamera =
gameObject.GetComponent<PerceptionCamera>();
     perceptionCamera.StartDataCapture();
   }
}
```

Unity Perception allows for the easy creation of synthetic datasets, helping AI developers tackle challenges related to data scarcity, diversity, and quality.

---

2. GANs (Generative Adversarial Networks): For Data Augmentation

Generative Adversarial Networks (GANs) are a type of neural network architecture used for generating realistic synthetic data, including images, videos, and text. GANs consist of two networks: a **generator**, which creates fake data, and a **discriminator**, which attempts to distinguish real data from the generated data. Over time, both networks improve, resulting in highly realistic synthetic data.

Why GANs?

- **Data Augmentation:** GANs can generate new data samples that resemble real data, which is especially useful for augmenting datasets with a limited number of examples. This can improve the performance of machine learning models, particularly in cases where data is scarce or difficult to obtain.
- **Realism:** GANs are capable of generating high-quality synthetic data that is indistinguishable

from real-world data, making them ideal for training models in fields like computer vision, healthcare, and natural language processing.

- **Flexible Applications:** GANs can be applied across a variety of domains, including creating synthetic medical images for training diagnostic models, generating realistic faces for computer vision applications, or producing text for language models.

Key Features:

- **Data Diversity:** GANs can create highly diverse data, even from limited real-world examples, helping to improve model generalization.
- **Real-Time Generation:** GANs can generate data in real-time, allowing for the dynamic creation of large datasets for continuous model training.
- **Style Transfer and Image Synthesis:** GANs are frequently used in tasks like image super-resolution, style transfer, and creating photorealistic images from sketches or low-quality inputs.

Example: In the medical field, GANs have been used to generate synthetic medical images, such as X-rays and MRIs, to train AI models for disease detection, especially in cases where obtaining real medical images might violate privacy regulations or be expensive.

GAN Example Code:

```
import tensorflow as tf
from tensorflow.keras import layers

# Simple GAN model for image generation
def build_generator():
    model = tf.keras.Sequential([
        layers.Dense(128, input_dim=100,
activation='relu'),
        layers.Dense(784, activation='sigmoid'),
        layers.Reshape((28, 28, 1))
    ])
    return model

generator = build_generator()
generated_image = generator(tf.random.normal([1,
100]))
```

By leveraging GANs, AI developers can augment datasets with high-quality synthetic data, enabling more robust models without needing massive amounts of real-world data.

---

3. DeepMind MuJoCo: Physics Simulation for AI Training

DeepMind MuJoCo (Multi-Joint dynamics with Contact) is a state-of-the-art physics engine designed for simulating environments that involve physical interactions, such as robots, vehicles, and other multi-body systems. MuJoCo is widely used in AI research to train reinforcement learning models, as it provides highly accurate and computationally efficient simulations of physics-based environments.

Why MuJoCo?

- **Realistic Physics Simulation:** MuJoCo simulates rigid body dynamics, friction, contact forces, and other complex physical phenomena with high precision, which is essential for training AI models in robotics and autonomous control.
- **Reinforcement Learning Training:** MuJoCo is particularly suited for reinforcement learning (RL) tasks, where an agent learns by interacting with its environment and receiving feedback (rewards). The engine provides a controlled environment where AI models can learn tasks like walking, picking up objects, or navigating.
- **Scalability:** MuJoCo is optimized for high-performance simulations and can run at real-time speeds, enabling the training of large-scale reinforcement learning models in a reasonable amount of time.

Key Features:

- **High-Fidelity Simulations:** MuJoCo's advanced physics engine allows for precise control over simulations, enabling detailed training of robots and other physical systems.
- **Customizable Environments:** Users can design custom environments for their AI agents to interact with, such as robotics tasks involving manipulation, locomotion, and object interaction.
- **Efficient Learning:** By using simulated environments, agents can practice and improve their skills without the need for real-world experimentation, which can be costly or dangerous.

Example: In robotics, MuJoCo is often used to simulate a robot learning to walk. By interacting with a simulated environment that replicates real-world physics, the robot can improve its performance over millions of training iterations, without any risk of damage.

MuJoCo Example Code:

```
import mujoco_py

# Load a model and create a simulation
model =
mujoco_py.load_model_from_path("robot_arm.xml")
```

```
sim = mujoco_py.MjSim(model)

# Control the robot in the simulation
sim.data.ctrl[0] = 1.0  # Apply a control signal to the
robot arm joint
sim.step()  # Step the simulation forward
```

MuJoCo allows researchers and developers to train reinforcement learning models in realistic, physics-based environments, enabling the development of advanced robotics and autonomous systems.

Conclusion

Synthetic data and AI simulation are transformative technologies that have become essential tools for AI development. **Unity Perception** enables the generation of realistic synthetic datasets, perfect for training computer vision models in a controlled environment. **Generative Adversarial Networks (GANs)** provide a powerful method for data augmentation, producing high-quality synthetic data that helps enhance model performance. Finally, **DeepMind MuJoCo** provides a highly accurate and efficient physics engine for training reinforcement learning models in realistic simulations. Together, these technologies help AI developers overcome the challenges of limited real-world data and create more robust, high-performing models that can be deployed in diverse environments.

Chapter 12: Quantum AI & Next-Gen AI

The convergence of quantum computing and artificial intelligence (AI) has the potential to revolutionize the way we approach complex problems. With traditional computing hitting its limits in certain domains, quantum computing offers new possibilities for solving problems that were previously intractable. This chapter explores the emerging field of **Quantum AI**, which combines the power of quantum mechanics with machine learning techniques to unlock the next generation of AI models. We'll dive into key tools and frameworks such as **PennyLane**, **Qiskit**, and **TensorFlow Quantum**, all of which enable the development of quantum-enhanced machine learning algorithms.

---

1. PennyLane: Quantum Machine Learning Framework

PennyLane is an open-source software library for quantum machine learning, quantum chemistry, and quantum optimization. Developed by Xanadu, PennyLane is designed to integrate quantum computing with classical machine learning frameworks, allowing for the creation of quantum-enhanced AI models.

Why PennyLane?

- **Quantum-Classical Hybrid Systems:**
  PennyLane is unique in that it allows for the
  creation of hybrid quantum-classical systems.
  This means that users can design machine
  learning models that incorporate both classical
  and quantum elements, leveraging the strengths
  of both.
- **Cross-Platform Support:** PennyLane supports a
  variety of quantum hardware backends,
  including simulators, quantum processors from
  companies like IBM, Microsoft, and Google, as
  well as its own quantum hardware.
- **Automatic Differentiation:** PennyLane
  integrates with popular machine learning
  frameworks like TensorFlow and PyTorch,
  enabling the use of quantum circuits in the
  same way one would use neural networks, and
  allows for gradient-based optimization using
  automatic differentiation.

Key Features:

- **Quantum Circuits as Layers:** PennyLane
  enables quantum circuits to be used as layers
  within classical neural networks, bringing the
  power of quantum states to the learning process.
- **Quantum Gradients:** PennyLane facilitates the
  calculation of gradients with respect to quantum

parameters, which is critical for training quantum machine learning models.

- **Interoperability with ML Libraries:** PennyLane easily integrates with TensorFlow, PyTorch, and other machine learning libraries, enabling seamless workflow transitions between classical and quantum operations.

Example: In quantum machine learning, PennyLane can be used to build models that take advantage of quantum entanglement and superposition, which can help improve classification and regression tasks beyond the capabilities of classical approaches.

PennyLane Example Code:

```
import pennylane as qml
from pennylane import numpy as np

# Define a quantum node
dev = qml.device("default.qubit", wires=2)

@qml.qnode(dev)
def circuit(x):
    qml.Hadamard(wires=0)
    qml.CNOT(wires=[0, 1])
    qml.RX(x, wires=0)
    return qml.expval(qml.PauliZ(0))

# Quantum machine learning function
def quantum_ml_function(x):
```

```
    return circuit(x)

# Example usage
result = quantum_ml_function(np.pi/4)
print(result)
```

PennyLane is an excellent tool for those looking to experiment with quantum machine learning and build hybrid systems that can take advantage of quantum speed-ups.

2. Qiskit: IBM's Quantum Computing Toolkit

Qiskit is an open-source quantum computing framework developed by IBM. It provides tools for building and simulating quantum circuits, running quantum algorithms, and performing quantum machine learning tasks on quantum processors. Qiskit enables developers to create quantum programs using Python, making it an accessible tool for AI researchers interested in quantum computing.

Why Qiskit?

- **Wide Compatibility:** Qiskit can run quantum programs on a variety of quantum processors, including IBM's quantum computers available via the IBM Quantum Experience cloud platform.
- **Extensive Libraries:** Qiskit includes several libraries tailored for different quantum

applications, including quantum information, quantum chemistry, and quantum machine learning. It also provides simulators for testing algorithms before running them on actual hardware.

- **Community and Documentation:** Qiskit has a large community and extensive documentation, making it easy for developers to get started with quantum computing and quantum AI.

Key Features:

- **Quantum Circuits:** Qiskit provides tools for designing quantum circuits that can implement a wide range of quantum algorithms, from simple logic gates to complex quantum machine learning models.
- **Quantum Algorithms:** Qiskit includes implementations of key quantum algorithms like Grover's search algorithm, Shor's algorithm, and quantum phase estimation, which are critical for quantum-enhanced AI.
- **Cloud Integration:** Qiskit allows users to run quantum programs on IBM's cloud-based quantum processors, giving developers access to real quantum hardware for their AI experiments.

Example: Quantum machine learning algorithms, such as **Quantum Support Vector Machines (QSVM),**

can be implemented using Qiskit to solve classification problems more efficiently by leveraging quantum speed-ups in high-dimensional data spaces.

Qiskit Example Code:

```
from qiskit import Aer, transpile, assemble
from qiskit.visualization import plot_histogram
from qiskit import QuantumCircuit

# Create a simple quantum circuit
qc = QuantumCircuit(2)
qc.h(0)
qc.cx(0, 1)
qc.measure_all()

# Simulate the circuit
simulator = Aer.get_backend('qasm_simulator')
compiled_circuit = transpile(qc, simulator)
result =
simulator.run(assemble(compiled_circuit)).result()

# Display the result
counts = result.get_counts()
plot_histogram(counts)
```

Qiskit's flexibility and community support make it a powerful tool for AI researchers interested in exploring quantum computing and its applications in machine learning.

3. TensorFlow Quantum: Deep Learning for Quantum AI

TensorFlow Quantum (TFQ) is a library developed by Google that extends TensorFlow to enable quantum machine learning. It allows the integration of quantum computing into deep learning workflows, enabling the design and training of quantum neural networks (QNNs) on quantum processors.

Why TensorFlow Quantum?

- **Seamless Integration with TensorFlow:** TensorFlow Quantum extends TensorFlow, one of the most widely used machine learning frameworks, making it easy to combine classical deep learning models with quantum-enhanced models. This integration enables developers to work with existing machine learning pipelines and workflows.
- **Hybrid Models:** TFQ is particularly suited for creating hybrid models that combine quantum circuits with classical neural networks, allowing for quantum-enhanced feature extraction, classification, and regression tasks.
- **Quantum Circuit Representation:** TFQ provides tools for representing quantum circuits and integrating them into neural network

architectures, enabling the training of models that take advantage of quantum computation.

Key Features:

- **Quantum-Classical Hybrid Training:** TensorFlow Quantum allows for training hybrid quantum-classical models, where quantum circuits can serve as layers in a classical neural network, making it easier to incorporate quantum advantages into classical learning tasks.
- **Custom Quantum Layers:** TFQ supports the use of quantum layers, where quantum circuits are optimized alongside classical layers, providing a mechanism for quantum-enhanced learning in deep neural networks.
- **Access to Quantum Hardware:** TensorFlow Quantum can run quantum programs on simulators and quantum processors, providing real quantum hardware for testing and running quantum models.

Example: Using TensorFlow Quantum, AI models can be trained to classify complex data, such as images, by utilizing quantum circuits for feature extraction, which could offer significant advantages in tasks that require high-dimensional data processing.

TensorFlow Quantum Example Code:

```
import tensorflow as tf
import tensorflow_quantum as tfq
import cirq

# Define a simple quantum circuit
qubits = cirq.LineQubit.range(2)
circuit = cirq.Circuit(
    cirq.H(qubits[0]),
    cirq.CNOT(qubits[0], qubits[1]),
    cirq.measure(qubits[0], qubits[1])
)

# Convert the circuit to a tensor
quantum_data = tfq.convert_to_tensor([circuit])

# Define a simple quantum model
model = tf.keras.Sequential([
    tfq.layers.PQC(circuit, tf.keras.layers.Dense(1))
])

# Compile and train the model
model.compile(optimizer=tf.keras.optimizers.Adam(),
loss='mean_squared_error')
model.fit(quantum_data, y=[1.0])
```

TensorFlow Quantum makes it easier to design, train, and deploy quantum-enhanced AI models, leveraging the powerful tools and community that TensorFlow already provides.

Conclusion

Quantum AI represents the next frontier in machine learning, with the potential to solve problems that are computationally infeasible for classical computers. Tools like **PennyLane**, **Qiskit**, and **TensorFlow Quantum** are key to developing quantum-enhanced AI models, enabling researchers to harness the power of quantum computing for applications ranging from optimization and classification to simulation and drug discovery. By integrating quantum mechanics with machine learning techniques, we can unlock new levels of computational power and drive forward the capabilities of AI.

Chapter 13: AI Security & Ethical AI

As AI systems become increasingly embedded in our daily lives and critical decision-making processes, ensuring their security, fairness, and transparency becomes more important than ever. This chapter focuses on the ethical concerns and security issues surrounding AI and presents tools and frameworks that help address these challenges. We will explore solutions such as **IBM AI Fairness 360**, **Adversarial Robustness Toolbox (ART)**, and **Explainable AI (XAI)** techniques like **SHAP** and **LIME**.

---

1. IBM AI Fairness 360: Detecting and Mitigating Bias in AI Models

IBM AI Fairness 360 (AIF360) is an open-source toolkit designed to help developers and data scientists detect and mitigate bias in machine learning models. Bias in AI models can have serious consequences, especially in high-stakes domains such as healthcare, hiring, law enforcement, and finance. AIF360 provides a comprehensive set of tools for fairness assessment, enabling practitioners to ensure that their AI models are both accurate and equitable.

Why AI Fairness 360?

- **Fairness Metrics:** The toolkit includes over 70 fairness metrics for classification and regression tasks, which help evaluate the performance of AI models with respect to different demographic groups (e.g., gender, race, age).
- **Bias Mitigation Algorithms:** AIF360 offers a range of algorithms that can be applied to datasets and models to reduce bias, including pre-processing, in-processing, and post-processing techniques.
- **Customizable and Extensible:** The library allows for easy customization and integration with existing machine learning workflows, making it a versatile tool for fairness evaluation.

Key Features:

- **Bias Detection:** AIF360 can analyze the outputs of machine learning models to identify potential sources of bias, providing insights into where disparities might exist between different demographic groups.
- **Fairness Mitigation Techniques:** The toolkit offers various algorithms like **Reweighing**, **Disparate Impact Remover**, and **Adversarial Debiasing** to mitigate bias before, during, or after the model training process.
- **Visualization Tools:** AIF360 includes visualization tools that provide visual insights

into fairness and bias, helping users make data-driven decisions about how to improve their models.

Example Use Case: In a loan approval system, AIF360 can be used to assess the fairness of the AI model by analyzing whether the model is biased against applicants from certain demographic groups. If bias is detected, users can apply fairness mitigation techniques to ensure equitable outcomes.

Example Code:

```
from aif360.datasets import BinaryLabelDataset
from aif360.metrics import BinaryLabelDatasetMetric
from aif360.algorithms.preprocessing import
Reweighing

# Load dataset
dataset = BinaryLabelDataset(df=df,
label_names=['loan_approval'],
protected_attribute_names=['gender'])

# Evaluate fairness metrics
metric = BinaryLabelDatasetMetric(dataset,
privileged_groups=[{'gender': 1}],
unprivileged_groups=[{'gender': 0}])
print('Statistical parity difference:',
metric.statistical_parity_difference())

# Apply reweighing to mitigate bias
```

```
reweighing = Reweighing()
dataset_transf = reweighing.fit_transform(dataset)
```

IBM AI Fairness 360 is a powerful resource for developers working to build AI systems that are not only effective but also fair and responsible.

---

2. Adversarial Robustness Toolbox (ART): Protecting AI from Adversarial Attacks

Adversarial Robustness Toolbox (ART) is an open-source library that provides tools for defending machine learning models against adversarial attacks. Adversarial attacks involve manipulating input data in subtle ways that can lead to incorrect predictions or classifications by AI systems. These attacks pose significant risks, especially in domains such as autonomous vehicles, healthcare, and finance.

Why ART?

- **Comprehensive Attack Detection:** ART provides a wide range of adversarial attack methods, allowing practitioners to evaluate the robustness of their models against various types of threats.
- **Defense Strategies:** The toolbox also includes techniques for defending against adversarial attacks, ensuring that AI models remain secure even when confronted with malicious input.

- **Scalability and Flexibility:** ART is designed to be flexible and scalable, making it suitable for both research and production environments. It supports a variety of machine learning frameworks, including TensorFlow, PyTorch, and Keras.

Key Features:

- **Adversarial Attacks:** ART supports different types of adversarial attacks, such as **FGSM (Fast Gradient Sign Method)**, **PGD (Projected Gradient Descent)**, and **DeepFool**, enabling users to test how vulnerable their models are.
- **Robustness Metrics:** The library includes various metrics to evaluate the robustness of machine learning models, helping developers quantify how resistant their models are to adversarial manipulations.
- **Defensive Methods:** ART offers a suite of defense strategies such as **Adversarial Training**, **Gradient Masking**, and **Input Preprocessing**, which can help mitigate the impact of adversarial attacks.

Example Use Case: In a facial recognition system, ART can be used to test how easily adversarial images can trick the model into making incorrect identifications. If vulnerabilities are found, defensive methods like adversarial training can be applied to improve the system's resilience.

Example Code:

```
from art.attacks.evasion import FastGradientMethod
from art.classifiers import TensorFlowClassifier
import tensorflow as tf

# Load a pre-trained model
model = tf.keras.models.load_model('my_model.h5')
classifier = TensorFlowClassifier(model=model)

# Generate adversarial examples using FGSM
attack = FastGradientMethod(classifier, eps=0.1)
x_adv = attack.generate(x_test)

# Evaluate the model's performance on adversarial
examples
accuracy = classifier.evaluate(x_adv, y_test)
print("Accuracy on adversarial examples:", accuracy)
```

The Adversarial Robustness Toolbox is an essential resource for ensuring the security of AI models against adversarial threats.

---

3. Explainable AI (XAI) with SHAP and LIME: Interpreting AI Decisions

Explainable AI (XAI) is a field of AI research that focuses on making the decision-making process of AI models more transparent and understandable to humans. While deep learning models have shown great success, their "black-box" nature makes it difficult to interpret how they make decisions. Tools like **SHAP (Shapley Additive Explanations)** and **LIME (Local Interpretable Model-Agnostic Explanations)** are designed to provide explanations for model predictions, improving trust and accountability.

Why Explainable AI?

- **Building Trust:** By providing clear explanations for why a model made a certain decision, XAI helps users trust the outcomes and understand how the model arrived at its conclusions.
- **Improving Accountability:** In fields like healthcare and finance, understanding the reasoning behind AI decisions is critical for accountability, especially when the decisions affect human lives.
- **Model Debugging:** XAI tools can also help identify issues with AI models, such as bias or misinterpretations, which can be corrected to improve the model's performance and fairness.

Key Features:

- **SHAP:** SHAP values provide a unified measure of feature importance, explaining how each feature contributes to the model's output. This method is grounded in cooperative game theory and ensures a fair distribution of contribution among all features.

- **LIME:** LIME provides local explanations by approximating the behavior of a black-box model with a simpler, interpretable model (e.g., a decision tree) on a local region of the input space.
- **Model-Agnostic:** Both SHAP and LIME can be applied to any machine learning model, making them versatile tools for model interpretability.

Example Use Case: In a credit scoring model, SHAP can be used to explain why a particular applicant was denied a loan, identifying which features (e.g., income, credit history) had the most influence on the decision.

SHAP Example Code:

```
import shap
import xgboost
import pandas as pd

# Load dataset and train a model
data = pd.read_csv('credit_data.csv')
X = data.drop('target', axis=1)
y = data['target']
model = xgboost.XGBClassifier()
model.fit(X, y)

# Create a SHAP explainer
explainer = shap.TreeExplainer(model)
```

```
shap_values = explainer.shap_values(X)

# Visualize SHAP values
shap.summary_plot(shap_values, X)
```

LIME Example Code:

```
import lime
from lime.lime_tabular import LimeTabularExplainer

# Train a classifier and prepare data
classifier = LogisticRegression()
classifier.fit(X_train, y_train)

# Initialize LIME explainer
explainer = LimeTabularExplainer(X_train.values,
training_labels=y_train.values, mode='classification')

# Explain a single prediction
exp = explainer.explain_instance(X_test.iloc[0],
classifier.predict_proba)
exp.show_in_notebook()
```

XAI tools like SHAP and LIME play a vital role in demystifying AI models and improving their transparency, making it easier to understand and trust their decisions.

Conclusion

AI security and ethics are essential considerations as AI systems are increasingly deployed in high-stakes and sensitive environments. Tools like **IBM AI Fairness 360**, **Adversarial Robustness Toolbox (ART)**, and **Explainable AI (XAI)** frameworks like **SHAP** and **LIME** help ensure that AI models are fair, secure, and interpretable. By addressing biases, protecting against adversarial attacks, and providing transparency into decision-making processes, these tools contribute to the responsible and ethical development of AI systems that can be trusted by society.

Chapter 14: Low-Code/No-Code AI Tools

Low-code and no-code AI tools are revolutionizing how individuals and businesses can leverage AI technology without requiring extensive coding knowledge or expertise in machine learning. These tools provide user-friendly interfaces, templates, and pre-built models to help users quickly build, train, and deploy AI models. This chapter will explore three prominent low-code/no-code AI platforms: **Google AutoML**, **Lobe by Microsoft**, and **RunwayML**. These platforms are democratizing AI development, making it accessible to a broader range of users—from small businesses to creatives.

---

1. Google AutoML: Build AI Models Without Coding

Google AutoML is a suite of machine learning products that allows developers, data scientists, and even non-technical users to train custom AI models without needing to write complex code. Using AutoML, users can create custom models tailored to specific tasks like image recognition, natural language processing, and structured data analysis.

Why Google AutoML?

- **Ease of Use:** Google AutoML's user-friendly interface simplifies the entire machine learning pipeline. Users can upload their data, define the problem, and the platform automatically selects the best algorithms and configurations for training the model.

- **Pre-Built Models:** AutoML provides pre-trained models that can be fine-tuned with user-specific data. This allows users to leverage existing, high-quality models without having to start from scratch.
- **Scalability:** Google AutoML integrates seamlessly with Google Cloud, offering powerful scalability for training and deployment. It's suitable for both small projects and large enterprise-scale applications.

Key Features:

- **Automated Model Selection and Tuning:** AutoML handles the selection of algorithms, hyperparameters, and model training, saving users time and effort in model development.
- **Customizable Models:** Although the platform is no-code, users can still adjust certain parameters to fine-tune their models for more specific use cases.
- **Integrated with Google Cloud:** Once models are trained, Google AutoML integrates smoothly with Google Cloud services like Google Cloud Storage and Google Kubernetes Engine for easy deployment.

Example Use Case: A small e-commerce company can use Google AutoML to build a custom image classification model for recognizing product categories (e.g., shirts, shoes, accessories) without needing a data science team.

Example Code:

```
from google.cloud import automl_v1beta1 as automl

# Initialize client for AutoML Vision
client = automl.AutoMlClient()

# Define the project and model details
project_id = 'your-project-id'
model_id = 'your-model-id'
model_full_id = client.model_path(project_id, 'us-central1', model_id)

# Predict on an image
prediction_client = automl.PredictionServiceClient()
file_path = 'path_to_image.jpg'

with open(file_path, 'rb') as content:
    image = {'image_bytes': content.read()}

# Get predictions
response =
prediction_client.predict(name=model_full_id,
payload={'image': image})
print(response)
```

Google AutoML simplifies the complexities of AI model training, providing an easy entry point for users to build and deploy models in a fraction of the time.

2. Lobe (Microsoft): No-Code AI Model Training for Image Recognition

Lobe is a no-code AI tool from Microsoft designed for training image recognition models without any programming knowledge. With Lobe, users can build custom AI models by simply uploading images and labeling them. The platform uses a drag-and-drop interface, making it easy for beginners to create models tailored to specific image classification tasks.

Why Lobe?

- **No-Code, No Complexity:** Lobe's interface is intuitive, enabling users to train custom image classifiers without needing any coding experience. The tool handles the complexity of machine learning behind the scenes.
- **Pre-Trained Models and Auto-Tuning:** Lobe provides pre-built model architectures and fine-tunes them automatically based on the uploaded data, optimizing them for the specific task at hand.
- **Deployment Made Easy:** Once the model is trained, Lobe allows users to export the model

for deployment in a variety of formats, including TensorFlow, ONNX, and CoreML, which makes it easy to integrate with other applications.

Key Features:

- **Drag-and-Drop Interface:** Users can upload images and label them by simply dragging and dropping them into the interface, making the training process extremely straightforward.
- **Automatic Model Training:** Lobe automatically trains a model based on the provided data, optimizing it for classification accuracy.
- **Cross-Platform Deployment:** Once trained, models can be exported to multiple formats, making it easy to integrate them into web, mobile, or desktop applications.

Example Use Case: A local farm can use Lobe to train a custom image recognition model to detect and classify different types of crops (e.g., tomatoes, carrots, lettuce) for automatic harvest tracking.

Example Workflow:

1. Upload images of different crops.
2. Label the images according to their category (e.g., Tomato, Lettuce, Carrot).
3. Let Lobe automatically train the model.

4. Export the model to a mobile app to identify crops in real time.

---

3. RunwayML: AI-Powered Creative Applications

RunwayML is a powerful AI platform tailored for creatives, allowing artists, designers, and developers to access state-of-the-art AI models for various creative applications without writing code. RunwayML offers an extensive library of pre-trained models for tasks like image manipulation, text generation, video editing, and style transfer. It provides a no-code environment that integrates seamlessly with creative software like Adobe Photoshop and Unity, making it a go-to tool for those working in the creative industry.

Why RunwayML?

- **Creative Focus:** Unlike other no-code AI platforms that focus on traditional business applications, RunwayML is specifically designed for the creative community. It helps artists and designers leverage AI for innovative projects.
- **Real-Time Collaboration:** RunwayML supports real-time collaboration, enabling teams to work together on creative AI projects.
- **Extensive Library of AI Models:** The platform offers a broad selection of pre-trained models for

various creative tasks, including generating artwork, manipulating video, and creating animations.

Key Features:

- **AI for Artists:** RunwayML includes models for creative tasks such as generating art, automating video editing, and creating text-based content (e.g., poetry or stories).
- **Integration with Creative Tools:** The platform integrates with popular creative software like Adobe Photoshop, Premiere Pro, and Unity, allowing users to enhance their existing workflows with AI.
- **Real-Time Interaction:** Users can interact with AI models in real time, making it possible to experiment and iterate creatively on the fly.

Example Use Case: A filmmaker could use RunwayML to create realistic visual effects, such as face swaps, deepfakes, or text-to-image transformations, in real time during production.

Example Workflow:

1. Choose a pre-trained model (e.g., style transfer or text-to-image generation).
2. Import the media (images or videos) that need to be enhanced or manipulated.

3. Adjust settings, such as the style for artistic effects or the text prompt for image generation.
4. Use the real-time output to immediately see how the AI model transforms the media.

Conclusion

Low-code/no-code AI tools are empowering a wide range of individuals—from small business owners to creatives—to tap into the power of artificial intelligence without the need for extensive coding knowledge. **Google AutoML**, **Lobe by Microsoft**, and **RunwayML** offer intuitive platforms for building custom models, training image classifiers, and exploring AI-powered creative applications. These tools are making AI more accessible than ever before, enabling users to develop innovative solutions and enhance their workflows in an easy, efficient, and impactful way. Whether you're interested in creating a business AI model, enhancing creative projects, or exploring machine learning for fun, these tools provide a gateway to the world of AI without requiring any technical expertise.

Chapter 15: AI Research & Open-Source Communities

AI research and open-source communities play a vital role in advancing the field of artificial intelligence, fostering collaboration, innovation, and the sharing of knowledge. This chapter explores three essential platforms for AI researchers and developers: **ArXiv**, **Papers With Code**, and **Fast.ai**. These platforms provide valuable resources for staying up-to-date with the latest developments in AI research, accessing state-of-the-art models and code implementations, and learning through high-level deep learning courses. By leveraging these platforms, individuals can contribute to and learn from the AI community while enhancing their own projects and knowledge.

---

1. ArXiv: Stay Updated with the Latest AI Research Papers

ArXiv is a free and open-access repository that hosts research papers in various fields, including computer science, physics, mathematics, and more. The AI section of ArXiv is a critical resource for researchers, practitioners, and enthusiasts who want to stay updated with the latest advancements in artificial intelligence. Whether you're looking for papers on deep learning, reinforcement learning, natural language processing (NLP), or generative models, ArXiv is a comprehensive source for peer-reviewed and preprint publications.

Why ArXiv?

- **Access to Cutting-Edge Research:** ArXiv hosts the most up-to-date research papers, allowing users to access the latest work in AI before it's formally published in journals or conferences.
- **Free and Open Access:** ArXiv is open to everyone, with no subscription fees, making it a valuable resource for researchers, students, and anyone interested in AI development.
- **Wide Range of Topics:** The AI section on ArXiv covers a vast array of subfields, including machine learning, computer vision, NLP, robotics, ethics in AI, and more, ensuring that users have access to diverse topics within AI research.

Key Features:

- **Preprints and Peer-Reviewed Papers:** ArXiv allows researchers to share preprints, making their work accessible to the community before official peer review. It also hosts peer-reviewed journals for established research.
- **Search and Filter:** ArXiv has powerful search and filtering tools, allowing users to narrow down results based on keywords, authors, or publication dates.

- **Cross-Disciplinary Research:** ArXiv covers many areas related to AI, such as mathematics, neuroscience, and computational theory, helping researchers explore interdisciplinary connections.

Example Use Case: An AI researcher interested in the latest advancements in reinforcement learning can use ArXiv to search for and read papers related to novel algorithms or applications of reinforcement learning in robotics.

Example Workflow:

1. Visit the **AI Section** on ArXiv.
2. Use the search bar to find research papers related to a specific AI topic (e.g., "transformers in NLP").
3. Filter the results by publication date to ensure you're viewing the latest papers.
4. Download or read papers to stay updated with recent developments in the field.

---

2. Papers With Code: AI Models with Implementation Details

Papers With Code is a platform that connects research papers with the code that implements the algorithms or models described in those papers. It is an invaluable resource for AI researchers and practitioners who want to understand how a specific AI model works in practice and explore real-world implementations. By linking research papers to open-source code repositories, Papers With Code accelerates the adoption of new techniques and helps users replicate results, experiment with models, and improve upon existing solutions.

Why Papers With Code?

- **Implementation Details:** Papers With Code offers detailed code implementations for many popular AI papers, helping users bridge the gap between theory and practice.
- **Benchmarking and Performance Metrics:** The platform provides performance benchmarks for different AI models, allowing users to compare them and select the best one for their application.
- **Collaboration and Innovation:** By open-sourcing the code and linking it with research papers, the platform fosters collaboration, enabling the AI community to iterate and build upon each other's work.

Key Features:

- **Code Repositories:** Links to GitHub repositories or other platforms where the code for a specific model is available, allowing users to experiment with and adapt the model to their needs.

- **Model Performance Benchmarks:** Provides tables and rankings of AI models based on various performance metrics, so users can quickly assess the strengths and weaknesses of different approaches.
- **Trending Models and Papers:** Features a section for the most popular papers and models, helping users stay informed about the hottest topics and breakthroughs in AI.

Example Use Case: A developer working on a natural language processing task can use Papers With Code to find a recent paper on transformers, access the accompanying code implementation, and replicate the results for their own project.

Example Workflow:

1. Visit **Papers With Code** and use the search bar to find a specific AI paper (e.g., "BERT for sentiment analysis").
2. Explore the code implementations linked to the paper, and review the performance metrics.
3. Clone the GitHub repository to test and adapt the model to your own data.
4. Contribute back by improving the model and sharing your modifications with the community.

3. Fast.ai: High-Level AI Research and Deep Learning Courses

Fast.ai is an educational platform that provides deep learning courses, research papers, and tools for AI practitioners. The goal of Fast.ai is to make deep learning more accessible to people with diverse backgrounds, from beginners to advanced researchers. The platform offers a top-down approach to learning AI, where students start building powerful models right away and learn the underlying theory as they go.

Why Fast.ai?

- **Practical, Hands-On Learning:** Fast.ai's courses focus on practical deep learning applications, enabling learners to quickly build and deploy models, even without extensive mathematical knowledge.
- **State-of-the-Art Techniques:** The platform covers cutting-edge AI techniques and research, helping learners stay ahead of the curve and implement the latest advancements in deep learning.
- **Community-Driven:** Fast.ai has a vibrant and supportive community that actively contributes to the platform, creating a collaborative learning environment.

Key Features:

- **Free Courses and Tutorials:** Fast.ai offers free courses on deep learning, machine learning, and AI, with a focus on making these topics accessible to everyone.
- **High-Level API:** Fast.ai provides a high-level API built on top of PyTorch, enabling users to implement deep learning models with minimal code and effort.
- **Research Papers and Code:** Fast.ai also provides links to key research papers and their corresponding code implementations, similar to Papers With Code, but with an emphasis on learning by doing.

Example Use Case: A student who is new to deep learning can use Fast.ai's course on practical deep learning to build their first neural network, understand how to fine-tune models, and gain a deeper understanding of advanced topics like transfer learning and computer vision.

Example Workflow:

1. Enroll in Fast.ai's **Practical Deep Learning for Coders** course.
2. Follow along with the course material, building models on image classification or text processing.

3. Apply techniques such as transfer learning to improve model performance without needing a vast dataset.
4. Participate in the Fast.ai forums to ask questions, share progress, and collaborate with other learners.

Conclusion

AI research and open-source communities are essential to the advancement of artificial intelligence. Platforms like **ArXiv**, **Papers With Code**, and **Fast.ai** are helping to accelerate the dissemination of research, the implementation of AI models, and the accessibility of deep learning education. By utilizing these resources, AI practitioners can stay informed about the latest advancements, access open-source code for research and practical implementation, and continue to learn from high-quality, hands-on educational content. These platforms not only support individual growth but also foster collaboration within the global AI community.

Final Takeaways & Execution Strategy

As you embark on your AI journey, it's important to have a clear roadmap to help guide you from learning the basics to building your own AI projects. Here's a breakdown of a strategic approach for beginners to get started with AI and machine learning (ML):

For Beginners:

1. **Learn Python**
   - **Why Python?** Python is the most widely used language for AI and ML development due to its simplicity and vast ecosystem of libraries. It is beginner-friendly and allows for rapid development of AI models.
   - **How to Start:**
     - Familiarize yourself with Python basics: variables, data types, control flow, and functions.
     - Use free online resources such as Codecademy, Coursera, or edX to learn Python.
2. **Master Core Libraries (Pandas & NumPy)**
   - **Pandas**: A powerful library for data manipulation and analysis. Pandas allows you to easily work with structured data, such as datasets in CSV or Excel format.

- o **NumPy**: The foundation for numerical computing in Python. It's essential for handling arrays and performing mathematical operations on large datasets.
- o **How to Start:**
  - Work on basic data manipulation tasks like cleaning data, sorting, filtering, and summarizing information.
  - Solve small challenges on platforms like Kaggle to practice your Pandas and NumPy skills.

3. **Learn Deep Learning Frameworks (TensorFlow/PyTorch)**
   - o **TensorFlow**: Developed by Google, TensorFlow is a powerful and flexible deep learning framework. It's ideal for both beginners and advanced users looking to build machine learning models.
   - o **PyTorch**: Developed by Facebook, PyTorch is known for its flexibility and ease of use, especially in research and experimentation.
   - o **How to Start:**
     - Begin by learning the basics of TensorFlow or PyTorch by following beginner tutorials and documentation on their official websites.

- Implement basic models like linear regression, classification, and simple neural networks.

4. **Try Hugging Face Models for LLMs and NLP**
   - **Hugging Face** provides pre-trained models for natural language processing (NLP) tasks like text classification, translation, summarization, and even conversational agents (chatbots).
   - **Why Hugging Face?**
     - The Hugging Face Model Hub offers easy-to-use models and APIs for NLP tasks, making it simple to experiment with large language models (LLMs) like GPT, BERT, and others.
     - The platform is beginner-friendly and comes with extensive documentation, making it easy to integrate models into your applications.
   - **How to Start:**
     - Use the Hugging Face Transformers library to fine-tune pre-trained models for specific NLP tasks.
     - Start by running pre-built examples and experiment with your own datasets.

5. **Start Building Small AI Projects**
   - **Project Examples:**

- **Chatbots**: Build simple chatbots using NLP models, which can be integrated into websites or apps for customer service.
- **Image Classifiers**: Create basic image classification models using TensorFlow or PyTorch to classify images from popular datasets like MNIST or CIFAR-10.
- **Recommendation Systems**: Develop a recommendation engine that suggests products, movies, or music based on user preferences.

- **Why Start with Projects?**
  - Building small projects allows you to apply the knowledge you've gained, gain hands-on experience, and solidify your understanding of AI concepts.
  - Projects will also make your portfolio more attractive to potential employers or collaborators.

- **How to Start:**
  - Pick a small project that aligns with your interests and goals. Use datasets from Kaggle or other online repositories.
  - Document your process, from collecting data to model training and deployment, and share your projects on GitHub to showcase your skills.

Execution Strategy

1. **Set Clear Learning Milestones:**
   - **1st Month**: Focus on learning Python and basic libraries like Pandas and NumPy.
   - **2nd Month**: Dive into TensorFlow or PyTorch, experimenting with simple neural networks and models.
   - **3rd Month**: Explore NLP with Hugging Face models and build your first chatbot or text classifier.
   - **4th Month and Beyond**: Start building real-world projects, such as recommendation systems, image classifiers, or chatbots, and experiment with more complex AI models.
2. **Consistency is Key:**
   - Allocate a specific amount of time each day or week to practice coding and working on AI concepts. Even 1-2 hours per day can make a significant difference over time.
   - Break complex tasks into manageable steps and gradually increase the difficulty of your projects as your skills improve.
3. **Join AI Communities:**
   - Participate in online communities like Reddit's r/MachineLearning, Stack Overflow, or Kaggle. Engage with other

learners, ask questions, and share your progress.

- o Collaborate on open-source projects to gain experience working in teams and learn best practices.

4. **Keep Updated with AI Trends:**
    - o Follow AI research on platforms like **ArXiv** and **Papers With Code** to stay up-to-date with the latest advancements in the field.
    - o Experiment with new frameworks and libraries as they are released to expand your knowledge and stay ahead in the field.

By following this execution strategy, you will be able to progress from a beginner to a proficient AI practitioner in a structured and manageable way. AI is a vast and evolving field, so continual learning, experimentation, and project-building are key to mastering it.

Advanced AI Strategy & Execution for Advanced Users

For advanced users who have already mastered the foundational skills in AI and machine learning, it's time to dive into more complex concepts and tools. Here's a roadmap for taking your AI expertise to the next level by building powerful AI systems, optimizing performance, and deploying models at scale.

For Advanced Users:

1. **Build Custom LLM-powered AI Agents with LangChain**
   - **Why LangChain?**
     - LangChain is a framework designed for building language model-powered applications. It enables you to integrate large language models (LLMs) into more complex workflows, such as information retrieval, summarization, and advanced NLP applications.
     - LangChain is ideal for building conversational agents, data-processing systems, and decision-making tools that require interaction with LLMs.
   - **How to Start:**

- Begin by familiarizing yourself with LangChain's core components, such as **Chains**, **Agents**, and **Prompts**.
- Build small prototypes using LangChain, such as an AI agent that fetches real-time data, processes it using an LLM, and performs actions based on the result.
- Experiment with integrating LangChain with external APIs, databases, and data pipelines to enhance the capabilities of your AI agents.

2. **Optimize AI Inference Using TensorRT & ONNX Runtime**
   - **Why TensorRT & ONNX Runtime?**
     - **TensorRT** is NVIDIA's high-performance deep learning inference optimizer, focused on optimizing models for deployment on NVIDIA GPUs. It can significantly improve inference speed and reduce latency, making it ideal for real-time AI applications.
     - **ONNX Runtime** is an open-source cross-platform inference engine that supports models trained in various frameworks (PyTorch, TensorFlow, Scikit-learn, etc.). ONNX enables you to optimize and run AI models

on multiple hardware platforms efficiently.

- How to Start:
  - Convert models trained in PyTorch or TensorFlow to the **ONNX format**, which is compatible with both ONNX Runtime and TensorRT.
  - Use **TensorRT** to perform post-training optimization, reducing memory usage and improving model inference speed on NVIDIA GPUs.
  - For **ONNX Runtime**, experiment with model acceleration on CPU, GPU, or even specialized hardware such as FPGAs for edge devices or embedded systems.
  - Compare performance improvements by benchmarking inference time before and after optimization with TensorRT or ONNX Runtime.

3. **Deploy AI Models in Production Using Docker + Kubernetes + MLflow**
   - **Why This Stack?**
     - **Docker** enables you to package AI models and their dependencies into containers, making it easier to deploy and manage AI applications consistently across different environments (e.g., development, testing, production).

- **Kubernetes** (K8s) helps in orchestrating containerized applications at scale, automating deployment, scaling, and management of AI models in production. It provides load balancing, scaling, and monitoring for model deployments.
- **MLflow** is an open-source platform for managing the lifecycle of machine learning models, including experiment tracking, model packaging, deployment, and serving.

- **How to Start:**
  - **Containerization with Docker**: Package your AI models and their environment (libraries, dependencies, etc.) into a Docker container. Create a Dockerfile to automate the build process and ensure reproducibility.
  - **Deploy with Kubernetes**: Use Kubernetes to manage and scale the deployment of your Dockerized models. Create Kubernetes manifests or Helm charts to define how your models should run on the cluster.
  - **Model Lifecycle Management with MLflow**: Set up MLflow to track experiments, log model parameters,

and manage models' versions throughout their lifecycle. Use MLflow for packaging models into a standardized format and deploying them to production.

- **Monitor and Scale**: Once deployed, use Kubernetes to monitor the performance of your models, and scale them automatically based on traffic or resource usage. Leverage MLflow to track any changes or updates made to the models in production.
- **CI/CD Pipeline**: Implement a continuous integration/continuous deployment (CI/CD) pipeline using **GitLab** or **Jenkins** integrated with Docker, Kubernetes, and MLflow. This ensures that your models are always up-to-date and that changes are tested and deployed smoothly.

Execution Strategy

1. **Set Clear Milestones for Advanced Projects:**
   - **1st Month**: Master LangChain and build a small custom LLM-powered application.
   - **2nd Month**: Focus on optimizing AI models using TensorRT and ONNX

Runtime. Benchmark performance and analyze improvements.

- o **3rd Month**: Learn Docker, Kubernetes, and MLflow for production deployments. Work on deploying a model pipeline that can scale and be easily managed.

2. **Advanced Tools and Techniques:**
   - o **Integrate Advanced Frameworks**: Explore additional frameworks like **Ray** for distributed AI applications or **DeepSpeed** for large model optimization.
   - o **Experiment with Hybrid Models**: Combine traditional machine learning techniques with deep learning for specific use cases, such as recommender systems, time series forecasting, or AI-based decision support systems.

3. **Focus on Performance Optimization:**
   - o Work on profiling and optimizing the training process as well as inference time to improve the efficiency of your AI models.
   - o Explore hardware accelerators (e.g., GPUs, TPUs, FPGAs) and experiment with running AI models on these devices for significant performance gains.
   - o Test deployment strategies for low-latency, real-time applications, such as robotics or autonomous systems.

4. **Collaborate with Industry Leaders:**

- Contribute to open-source projects and research papers in advanced AI technologies.
- Join AI communities like **ArXiv**, **Papers With Code**, and **Kaggle** to stay updated with the latest research and best practices in advanced AI development.
- Network with other professionals and attend AI conferences to exchange ideas and keep up with cutting-edge technologies.

5. **Prepare for Real-World Deployments:**
   - Plan for production-level deployment: Focus on aspects like model monitoring, failure recovery, data drift, and system updates to ensure your AI models perform reliably in real-world scenarios.
   - Implement **A/B testing** for evaluating the performance of different model versions in production environments, ensuring optimal user experience and results.

By following these advanced strategies and execution plans, you'll be well-equipped to take on sophisticated AI projects, optimize performance, and deploy scalable AI systems that are ready for production environments. With a clear focus on tools like LangChain, TensorRT, Kubernetes, and MLflow, you'll build the expertise necessary to tackle even the most challenging AI use cases.

AI Engineer Strategy for Production-Ready Systems

For AI engineers working in production environments, the focus shifts to ensuring that AI systems are robust, scalable, and efficient at every stage of their lifecycle. This includes mastering MLOps tools, building multi-agent systems for automation, and exploring cutting-edge technologies like Edge AI and Quantum AI for the future of AI deployment. Here's a roadmap for progressing as an AI engineer in a production environment.

For AI Engineers in Production:

1. **Master MLOps Tools for Managing AI Lifecycles**
   - **Why MLOps?**
     - MLOps (Machine Learning Operations) is the practice of automating and streamlining the deployment, monitoring, and governance of machine learning models in production. It's crucial for scaling AI systems in an enterprise environment and ensuring that

models are continually monitored, updated, and optimized.

- ○ **Key Tools to Master:**
  - ▪ **MLflow**: For managing model lifecycle, tracking experiments, and serving models in production.
  - ▪ **Kubeflow**: Kubernetes-native platform for deploying and managing end-to-end ML workflows at scale.
  - ▪ **TensorFlow Extended (TFX)**: A production-ready platform for managing the entire ML pipeline, from data preprocessing to model deployment and monitoring.
  - ▪ **DVC (Data Version Control)**: Tool for versioning data, models, and experiments, ensuring reproducibility and traceability in MLOps workflows.
  - ▪ **Seldon**: A platform for deploying machine learning models at scale with monitoring, scaling, and A/B testing built-in.
- ○ **How to Start:**
  - ▪ Set up a CI/CD pipeline for continuous training, testing, and deployment using **Jenkins**, **GitLab CI**, or **GitHub Actions**.
  - ▪ Use **Kubeflow** to automate model deployment, scaling, and

management across cloud or on-prem environments.

- Implement monitoring and logging practices with tools like **Prometheus**, **Grafana**, or **Elasticsearch** to track model performance, data drift, and issues in real-time.

2. **Work on Multi-Agent AI Architectures for Automation**
   o **Why Multi-Agent Systems?**
     - Multi-agent systems (MAS) involve the coordination of multiple autonomous agents that work together to solve complex problems. These systems are essential for building scalable AI solutions in areas like autonomous vehicles, smart cities, and robotics, where several agents need to collaborate, share information, and make decisions collectively.
   o **Key Concepts to Explore:**
     - **Agent-based Modeling (ABM)**: A computational model for simulating interactions of agents within a given environment to observe complex behaviors and outcomes.
     - **Reinforcement Learning (RL)**: Specifically, **multi-agent reinforcement learning (MARL)**

where multiple agents learn and adapt their strategies through interaction with each other and their environment.

- **Collaborative Filtering**: AI agents working together to solve problems by sharing insights, data, or tasks, commonly used in recommendation systems and collective problem-solving.
- **Communication Protocols**: Developing mechanisms for agents to communicate, collaborate, and negotiate for task allocation (e.g., **MAS-based coordination** or **swarm intelligence**).

- **How to Start:**
  - Build a **multi-agent simulation environment** using frameworks like **OpenAI Gym** or **PySC2** (StarCraft II) for training agents.
  - Implement **cooperative strategies** where multiple agents can learn to work together through **multi-agent reinforcement learning** (MARL) algorithms.
  - Explore **real-world applications** of MAS in fields like robotics (autonomous teams), IoT (distributed sensor networks), and finance (AI trading agents).

3. **Experiment with Edge AI & Quantum AI for the Next-Gen Wave**
   - **Why Edge AI & Quantum AI?**
     - **Edge AI** involves running machine learning models on local devices (e.g., smartphones, embedded systems, IoT devices) rather than relying on centralized cloud infrastructure. This reduces latency, improves efficiency, and can be essential for real-time AI applications like autonomous vehicles, drones, and industrial robotics.
     - **Quantum AI** combines the power of quantum computing with AI techniques to solve problems that are intractable for classical computers. This is still an emerging field but promises breakthroughs in fields like optimization, drug discovery, cryptography, and materials science.
   - **Key Areas to Explore:**
     - **Edge AI Frameworks**: Platforms like **NVIDIA Jetson**, **Google Coral**, and **Intel OpenVINO** enable AI models to run efficiently on edge devices, handling local data processing, reducing cloud

dependence, and ensuring real-time performance.

- **Quantum AI Frameworks**: Experiment with quantum machine learning frameworks like **PennyLane**, **Qiskit**, and **TensorFlow Quantum** to explore how quantum circuits can improve AI tasks like data classification, optimization, and pattern recognition.

o **How to Start:**

- For **Edge AI**, develop and deploy AI models to edge devices such as Raspberry Pi, NVIDIA Jetson, or Google Coral. Experiment with lightweight models (e.g., **MobileNet**, **TinyML**) to optimize for constrained hardware.

- For **Quantum AI**, start by learning about **quantum algorithms** (e.g., **Grover's algorithm**, **Shor's algorithm**) and how they can be applied to AI problems. Use platforms like **Qiskit** or **PennyLane** to build quantum-inspired ML models.

- Work on **combining Edge AI and Quantum AI** by running classical AI models at the edge while simultaneously exploring how quantum computation can complement these systems for specialized tasks like optimization and simulation.

Execution Strategy for AI Engineers in Production

1. **Set Up MLOps Pipelines (1–2 Months):**
   - Begin by integrating MLOps tools such as **Kubeflow**, **MLflow**, and **DVC** to automate model lifecycle management, ensuring continuous integration and deployment in a production environment.
   - Establish monitoring practices to track model performance and manage versioning and experiments across teams.
2. **Develop Multi-Agent Systems (2–3 Months):**
   - Design and implement a basic multi-agent system with reinforcement learning or agent-based modeling techniques.
   - Scale the system by experimenting with different coordination strategies and applying them to real-world use cases like robotics, IoT, and automation.
3. **Explore Edge AI & Quantum AI (3–4 Months):**
   - Focus initially on deploying AI models to edge devices using frameworks like **NVIDIA Jetson** or **Google Coral**. Explore

optimization strategies for AI models to run efficiently on constrained hardware.

- o Experiment with **Quantum AI** by simulating quantum algorithms and understanding their potential impact on classical AI techniques, particularly in optimization and data processing tasks.

4. **Collaborate & Stay Current:**
   - o Collaborate with research groups and industry leaders working on cutting-edge technologies like Edge AI and Quantum AI.
   - o Stay up-to-date by following resources like **arXiv**, **Papers with Code**, and **AI research conferences** to explore new tools, methodologies, and trends in production AI systems.

By mastering MLOps tools, exploring multi-agent architectures, and experimenting with Edge AI and Quantum AI, AI engineers can ensure that their AI systems are future-proof, highly scalable, and ready for the demands of next-generation applications. These strategies provide the skills needed to build resilient AI systems in production that can adapt to future technological advancements.

Table of Contents